T0199156

According to His
PURPOSE

Volume I

Frederick A. Dowdell Sr.

WESTBOW
PRESS®
A DIVISION OF THOMAS NELSON
& ZONDERVAN

Scripture taken from the King James Version of the Bible.

WestBow Press books may be ordered through booksellers or by contacting:

WestBow Press
A Division of Thomas Nelson & Zondervan
1663 Liberty Drive
Bloomington, IN 47403
www.westbowpress.com
1 (866) 928-1240

ISBN: 978-1-5127-5841-2 (sc)
ISBN: 978-1-5127-5855-9 (hc)
ISBN: 978-1-5127-5840-5 (e)

Library of Congress Control Number: 2016916205

Print information available on the last page.

WestBow Press rev. date: 10/21/2016

About the Book

This book is mainly for new believers but can help seasoned believers of God's Word understand what he is speaking to us all. The book takes scriptures and breaks them down so that they are more understandable and easier to digest. Every scripture in the Bible is an inspiration of God and is profitable for doctrine, for reproof, for correction, for instruction in righteousness to help every believer understand who he is. We must all be doers and not just hearers of God Word. We must study God's Word and show ourselves approved.

CONTENTS

ACKNOWLEDGEMENTS

I would like to thank my Father, Savior and Lord, Jesus Christ for the inspiration to put together such a book for the new believer. I give all glory to God because without Him there would be no me and if He had not chosen me to write this book then it would not be. I would like to thank all my family and friends who have encouraged me to stay the path and complete this book but mostly my number one fan my wife, Rudeen Cecelia Dowdell (Sept. 6, 1969-Aug. 4 2016). Although she has passed on and went home to be with our Father, she is still an inspiration to my ongoing ministry that she helped build in me. I am truly blessed to have what God gave me as a compassionate, loving wife to encourage and push me beyond my means and to stick with me in the good, the bad and the ugly. No matter what anyone says luv, you will forever be in my heart. I truly miss and love you so much.

INTRODUCTION

In the Beginning

You see God created everything we needed in life. In the beginning when God created the heavens and the earths and the fullness there of was without void. The plants were created as food for the body and water for cleansing of the body. But before that He created the light and the dark which He separated, because both cannot dwell in the same place (Gen. 1). He also purposed men to write His words in what we now call the Bible. *All scripture is given by inspiration of God, and is profitable for doctrine, for reproof, for correction, for instruction in righteousness:* 2 Timothy 3:16. There are scripture in the Bible that has been set for you according to the purpose of God.

Throughout this book you will see words in italics and in red, those are scriptures or scripture references. All scriptures used in this book are from the King James Version.

CHAPTER 1

Your Path to Righteousness

Psalm 119:105 Thy word is a lamp unto my feet, and a light unto my path.

Let us first differentiate the meaning between "*lamp*" and "*light*". A lamp is used by night, by implication, it shines just enough light for the immediate area. Lamp is defined as follows: *to glisten, candle, a device for giving light, either one consisting of an electric bulb together with its holder and shade or cover, or one burning gas or a liquid fuel and consisting of a wick or mantle and a glass shade.* In contrast, the definition of light is defined as follows: *the natural agent that stimulates sight and makes things visible, luminary, bright, clear, daylight, sun.* Glisten also means to sparkle. So that means that the word of God in the form of a lamp unto our feet, sparkles. God's word, as a lamp, will shed sufficient light unto our feet with each and every step in our walk with the Lord, equipping us with what is necessary to walk without stumbling (or sinning). We will be able to see the obstacles, temptations and traps because of the sparkle by the lamp, to avoid falling or stumbling. As we seek the Kingdom of God we must know where we are at that given moment. Jesus said *"But seek ye first the kingdom of God, and his righteousness; and all these things shall be added unto you. Take therefore no thought for the morrow: for the morrow shall take thought for the things of itself. Sufficient unto the day is the evil thereof.* Matthew 6:33-34

We must understand our duty by the word of God whether it be by day (sunlight) or by night (lamp). The night (darkness) signifies adversity and the day (sunlight) signifies prosperity. The word *"path"* talks about our choices and course of life; the word *"feet"* talks about our actions. Our choices and direction depends on how we use the lamp (word of God). It is a means to stir up a man's spirit, and quicken him to obedience as if the word was written to him as a lamp to his feet and a light to his path. When we come to hear the word of God as it is directed to you personally so that it apprehends the truth as it is spoken to you, it will stir and awaken you to take heed to what is being said, it will stir you to obedience.

The word of God is like a torch or lamp to us as we walk through this world of darkness. Satan is king of this earthly world and we must be sober, *be vigilant; because your adversary the devil, as a roaring lion, walketh about, seeking whom he may devour:* 1 Peter 5:8. The word of God shows us the way; it prevents our stumbling over obstacles. Just as a lamp when it shines light in a dark room so does the word of God.

It keeps us from wandering off the path of righteousness and onto paths that would lead into danger or turn us away altogether from the path of life. *We have also a more sure word of prophecy; whereunto ye do well that ye take heed, as unto a light that shineth in a dark place, until the day dawn, and the day star arise in your hearts:* 2 Peter 1:19. As we are called to go out into the darkness of this world, we should never venture there without the light of God's word in our hearts. We should all use the word of God personally, practically and habitually to let it direct us in our daily lives.

If you look at Psalm 119: [106] *I have sworn, and I will perform it, that I will keep thy righteous judgments.* It speaks of an oath which is a commitment or promise to do something. We all have made a promise to do something and some of us have succeeded and some of us have failed. This oath is saying that this person will follow God's ways. Now we know that as long as we follow God's ways and do His will then blessings shall be upon us and we shall walk in the light and on the right path. Now if we choose to fall from following God's ways and will then walk in darkness and fall off the path that has been predestined for us. *For whom he did foreknow, he also did predestinate to be conformed to the image of his Son, that he might be the firstborn among many brethren* Romans 8:29.

The Bible says that in John 1: 4-5 *In him was life; and the life was the light of men. And the light shineth in darkness; and the darkness comprehended it not.* Jesus is our light that lives down inside us and He shines in any darkness, Jesus came to give His life for us. He came so that we could have life and have it more abundantly, John 10:10. Christ's death was so that our sins will be forgiven. Christ loves us so much that He gave His life for us and we must believe in Him and the God that sent Him. Christ is both the light and the lamp. Christ, being the word of God, is a great light to some and a lamp to others. To Peter, He was a light when the angel stood by him in the prison and the light shined about him; *And, behold, the angel of the Lord came upon him, and a light shined in the prison: and he smote Peter on the side, and raised him up, saying, Arise up quickly. And his chains fell off from his hands* Acts 12:7. To Paul, He was a light when it shined from heaven around him and he heard Christ say to him, "Saul, Saul, why persecutest thou me?" *And as he journeyed, he came near Damascus: and suddenly there shined round about him a light from heaven: And he fell to the earth, and heard a voice saying unto him, Saul, Saul, why persecutest thou me?* Acts 9:3-4.

What the word of God does is connect with the Holy Spirit that lives down inside all of us. Once the word of God is connected with the Holy Spirit there is a light that comes on and when that light is on, we discover things concerning God and ourselves, that which we could not otherwise have known; it shows us what is missing and what is dangerous. Our lives will be a dark place in deed without the word of God. When darkness settles down upon us, the word of our Lord, like a brightly lit lamp, reveals the way we should go. When we make choices without the word of God we sometimes place our lives and the lives of those that depend on us into a world of darkness. Now, what the Holy Spirit does from inside of us, it guides us to the word of God that we need in order to get our lamps lit, so we can see where we are going and not fall flat on our faces.

The nature of the word of God and the intention of giving it to the world is so that it will be a lamp unto your feet. It is a lamp that we can set up and take it into our hands for our own particular use. *For the commandment is a lamp; and the law is light; and reproofs of instruction are the way of life:* Proverbs 6:23. The commandment is a lamp that is kept burning by the Holy Spirit which is the oil in our lamps that is ignited by the word of God that will direct us in our choices of righteousness and the steps we take to get there. This shows us what our duty is, both towards God and man; by it, is the knowledge of sin: this informs what righteousness God requires of us; by the light of it we see our own deformities and infirmities, the imperfection of our disobedience, and that we need a better righteousness than our own to justify us in the sight of God, because it directs how we walk and what to do.

Back in the old English times when they had no light poles to light the streets, they had to carry lamps with them as they walked the streets. The lamps gave light to where they were walking so that they would not fall into the open sewers or fall over the piles of filth and waste that lined the streets. This is how some of us are living now in this dark and wicked world but without the lamps or in other words, without the word of God. We are just lost in this world and do not know the righteous way or how to walk in it. The word of God shines a light on us to reveal to us where we are and how we are to live in this world. The most practical benefit of scripture is guidance in the acts of our daily lives. The word of God is not sent to us so that we can be astonished by its true brilliance, but to guide and direct us by its instructions. *Happy is the man that findeth wisdom, and the man that getteth understanding* Proverbs 3:13. Believe it or not, we all need guidance and direction in order to live righteously in this dark and wicked world.

David was a man of intelligent humor and natural understanding, that was often afflicted; but with longing desires to become more holy offered daily prayers for quickening grace. He gives to God the glory of his wisdom, when he was not guided by the light of the word of God, his best light was but darkness. We walk in total darkness when we choose not to let the word of God shine down on us to direct us in all our ways. If you are walking in darkness surely, sooner or later you will stumble. David guided his steps by the word of God as if it was a lamp by night and a light by day. The word of God imparts heavenly knowledge that leads to righteous decisions and that is followed by determined resolution that brings with it great peace. If we consider; that if we hearken not to the word of God and if we walk not by the rule thereof, how is it possible we can come to the face of God?

David guided his own steps with the light of the lamp by night and its light by day. He saw the hard times of the road he traveled by the beams that shown from the lamp. Those that choose to continue to walk in darkness is sure to stumble, sooner or later. But those that choose to walk by the light during the day or by the lamp at night will not stumble but keep their up rightness.

Our journey is as important as our destination. It should be observed, that the word of God is only so to a man whose eyes are opened and enlightened by the Spirit of God, which is usually done by means of the word. A lamp or any other light are of no use to a blind man. We are in darkness and cannot see unless we are enlightened with the word of God. Not only does the word of God inform us of His Will, but as a light on a path of darkness, it shows us how to follow the right and avoid the wrong way. We should bless God for the light to guide us until the Son of Righteousness shall come, and we shall be made capable of seeing Him. *We have also a more sure word of prophecy; whereunto ye do well that ye take heed, as unto a light that shineth in a dark place, until the day dawn, and the day star arise in your hearts:* 2 Peter 1:19. *And they shall see his face; and his name shall be in their foreheads:* Revelation 22:4. The wicked will always try to lay traps to pull you from the righteous path that God has set for you, and to have our soul or life continually in our hands implies constant danger of life, but happy is the child of God that do not err from the Master's precepts. *My soul is continually in my hand: yet do I not forget thy law. The wicked have laid a snare for me: yet I erred not from thy precepts:* Psalm 119:109-110. The word of God is the light that shines in a dark and lonely place; it is a lamp to be carried by the believer, while they go *through* this dark and lonely place. The standard of Faith is that by the light of this lamp; the difference between true and false doctrine may be discerned, our error and immortality may be reproved and made manifest; the way of truth and godliness in which a man should walk is shown and he may see the stumbling blocks in his way and he can avoid the pitfalls and ditches.

Psalm 119: [113] I hate vain thoughts: but thy law do I love.
[114] Thou art my hiding place and my shield: I hope in thy word.
[115] Depart from me, ye evildoers: for I will keep the commandments of my God.
[116] Uphold me according unto thy word, that I may live: and let me not be ashamed of my hope.
[117] Hold thou me up, and I shall be safe: and I will have respect unto thy statutes continually.
[118] Thou hast trodden down all them that err from thy statutes: for their deceit is falsehood.
[119] Thou puttest away all the wicked of the earth like dross: therefore I love thy testimonies.
[120] My flesh trembleth for fear of thee; and I am afraid of thy judgments.

God has already predestined our walks in this life but we as humans defy what God has set for us by leaning unto our own understanding. *Trust in the LORD with all thine heart; and lean not unto thine own understanding* Proverbs 3:5. God has given us a light that shines on the path He has set for us, so that we may see the path and the dangers that may be on that path. When we decide to not walk the path God has set for us, we fall into total darkness and cannot see or understand anything that is on the path that we chose. When we lean unto the understanding of our Lord Jesus, we make the word of God our guide and its teachings are marked in the right way. We now clearly see the path and will be able to walk the path that we ought to go and avoid all those paths that will lead us astray. Now we can see the dangers that lie on the path that takes us to the right or left instead of the strait way. *Enter ye in at the strait gate: for wide is the gate, and broad is the way, that leadeth to destruction, and many there be which go in thereat: Because strait is the gate, and narrow is the way, which leadeth unto life, and few there be that find it* Matthew 7:33-34. We all need guidance and direction so why not take heed to the word of God and let it be a lamp unto your feet and a light unto your righteous path. *Wherewithal shall a young man cleanse his way? by taking heed thereto according to thy word* Psalm 119:9.

We know that this path that God has set for us is *the way* by which we will reach our destination, and it is *the truth* that leads us to *eternal life*, Jesus said in John 14: 6 *I am the way, the truth, and the life: no man cometh unto the Father, but by me.* There are many paths that turn off to the right or left, from our predestined path. Those paths lead to destruction. We have chosen the righteous path, which is not a path that we would choose naturally, even along this path God's word sparkles at our every step, as a lamp unto our feet, we are going to stumble because of our sinful nature. We should never ever give up but continue, a*nd make straight paths for your feet, lest that which is lame be turned out of the way; but let it rather be healed* Hebrews 12:13. There is always healing and

CHAPTER 2

No Respecter of Person

Acts 10:34 Then Peter opened his mouth, and said, Of a truth
I perceive that God is no respecter of persons:

As our Creator, God looks at each and every one of us as the
same person because He looks at us from the inside out. And
it is often said of God that he doth not respect persons. In an
ancient Near Eastern practice, when you greet a superior, you
lowered your face or sank to the earth. Now, if the superior
raised the face of the greeter, it was a sign of recognition and
esteem. God being the impartial judge in the Old Testament
showed no such favoritism, Deut. 10:17; 2 Chron. 19:7; Job
34:19; Rom. 2:11; Col. 3:25; 1 Pet. 1:17. Peter began his
sermon by declaring that God is impartial and shows no
favoritism of persons. His words that were spoken by Peter
says that He is *no respecter of persons.* This excellent speech
of Peter's is admirably suited to the circumstances of those

to whom he preached it; for it was a new sermon. Just as you read it, it is just what you needed to hear because we are respecter of persons unlike our Father. He does not give judgment in favor of any man for the sake of any external advantage. God never perverts judgment upon personal regards and considerations, nor countenances a wicked man in a wicked thing for the sake of his beauty, or stature, his country, parentage, relations, wealth, or honor in the world. He is *no respecter of persons*. God, as a benefactor, gives favors arbitrarily and by sovereignty Deut. 7:7, 8; 9:5, 6; Matt. 20:10; but he does not, as a judge, so give sentence; *but in every nation*, and under ever denomination, *he that fears God and works righteousness is accepted of him*, Acts 10:35. Peter applies this character quality to God's dealing with persons *from every nation (ethnos)*. This term refers not simply to nation-states but also to any racial, ethnic or cultural grouping by which humans distinguish themselves. Peter says that persons in every *ethnos* who fear God and do right are acceptable *(dektos)*, welcome, to him.

In Acts 10:35 Peter and Luke are seeking to avoid two extremes: The Jews' ethnic pride and prejudice, which saw no Gentile as a fit object of God's saving call, and the view that the religions of all cultures are equally valid bases for being acceptable to God. Although God has favored the Jews, above any other nation, He will never justify and save a wicked Jew that has lived and died unrepentant for their sins, even if they were *of the seed of Abraham*, and had all the honor and advantages of the circumcision. He does and will render *indignation and wrath, tribulation and anguish, upon every soul of man that doeth evil*; and *of the Jew first.* Rom. 2:3, 8, 9, 17. All power, both in heaven and in earth, is put into His hand, and all judgment committed to Him.

The honest Gentile, who has not the privileges and advantages that the Jews have, like Cornelius, who *fears God, and worships him, and works righteousness,* towards all men, will never be rejected or refused. God judges' men by their hearts, not by their country, heritage or parentage, and where there is an upright man, there is to be found an upright God, Psalms. 18:25. We are all accountable to Christ as our judge; so everyone must seek His favour, and to have Him as our friend.

Fearing God, and working righteousness, goes hand in hand, righteousness towards men is of true religion, so religion towards God is of righteousness. Godliness and honesty must go together. Where these are predominant, no doubt is to be made of the acceptance of God. No man can obtain the favor of God except through the mediation of Jesus Christ, and by the grace of God that is in him. Now, for those that do not have the knowledge of Him, and cannot have an explicit regard to Him, may yet receive grace from God for his sake, *to fear God and to work righteousness.* God gave Cornelius grace to do these things and through Christ, he was able to accept the work of his own hands. Though these are not the cause of a man's acceptance, yet they show it; and whatever may be wanting in knowledge or faith, will in due time be given by Him who has begun it.

According to what the writer of Hebrews was pointing out in 11:6, *Peter was saying the same thing: But without faith it is impossible to please him: for he that cometh to God must believe that he is, and that he is a rewarder of them that diligently seek him.*

Cornelius demonstrated belief in God's existence by turning away from idols and turning to the one true God and in turning away from pagan immorality to doing *what is right,* he showed his earnestness in seeking God. He had made the first steps of repentance. Now, this is not what saves him. Cornelius was a centurion, a position representing the heart and power of the Roman military and one of importance in the Roman world. It would have been impossible for Cornelius to have become a Jewish proselyte without losing his rank. Yet Cornelius was a God-fearer, as was his entire household (Acts 10:2). He was a devout God-fearer, even observing the Jewish hours of prayer in his home in such a manner as to be acceptable to God (Acts 3-4).

Only those who worship the one true God, and Jesus Christ that He sent, can know eternal life (John 17:3). While God prepared Peter for the border crossing (Acts 9-23), He had Cornelius send for Peter (Acts10:4-8). Peter's sermon shows us that God does not play favorites with nations, but he does make distinctions in matters of religion. Peter receives a vision that has both clean and unclean animals in it because he was troubled about the possibility of eating food prepared in the unclean home of Cornelius because he was a Gentile. The main illustration of the vision that Peter had was that Peter simply could have taken of the clean and left the unclean. The issue with Peter was the *mixing* of the clean with the unclean! Since Peter is *true to his religion*, he thinks that the unclean will taint the clean. God is showing Peter that the clean transforms the unclean. This is the same way that for those that have given their life to Christ (the clean) shall show those that are still living in the world (the unclean) what the Salvation of God looks and feels like. While Peter continues to think on the vision, the Holy Spirit tells him to go with the Gentiles that were asking for him at the gate. These were the Gentiles that Cornelius sent to bring Peter back to his home. As we know in the Christian movement, the crossing of the border from Jew to Gentile was not something that normally happens. But with God all things are possible and this is what God was showing with Cornelius and Peter. This is a major step for the Christian movement. This was a Spiritual intervention by God if you want to look at it that way. We as Christians must guard against prejudices so that we could see the good in all religions.

Peter said, *The word which God sent unto the children of Israel, preaching peace by Jesus Christ: (he is Lord of all:)* Acts 10:36. Before he could make a connection with his message or make an altar call God dealt with *the people of Israel,* by sending a message, *the Holy Ghost fell on all them which heard the word* Acts 10:44. God had just sent the Holy Spirit down upon all the God-fearers. The Jews were amazed at this point and could not argue with the reality of what God has done. God will go with those whom He anoints; He will be with those to whom He has given His spirit. This does not follow what

Peter spoke in Acts 2: 38 repent, and be baptized every one of you in the name of Jesus Christ for the remission of sins, and ye shall receive the gift of the Holy Ghost. The remission of sins lays a foundation for all other favours and blessings, by taking that out of the way which hinders the bestowing of them. If sin be pardoned, all is well, and shall end well for ever. The focus of attention was on the Jews that offered no resistance to Peter's suggestion that the God-fearers be baptized in the name of Jesus Christ. The Holy Ghost fell upon others after they were baptized, to confirm them in the faith; but upon these Gentiles before they were baptized, to show that God does not confine Himself to outward signs. The Holy Ghost fell upon those who were neither circumcised nor baptized; it is the Spirit that quickeneth, and the flesh profiteth nothing. Baptism was the first step for Gentiles to become Jewish proselytes (a person who has converted from one opinion, religion, or party to another) but was to be followed by circumcision. This was a major barrier crossed by Peter as the God-fearers were baptized into the Christian community without being circumcised. The kind of peace that Christ gave was not just for the Jews but for all people. It also was a peace that could tear down ethnic pride and the barriers of ethnic religious prejudice so that the Jews and Gentiles could live in harmony and be at peace with each other.

What Peter's sermon clearly shows is God's intention from the beginning of Christ's mission in Luke 2:10 *And the angel said unto them, Fear not: for, behold, I bring you good tidings of great joy, which shall be to all people.* Luke 2:14 *Glory to God in the highest, and on earth peace, good will toward men.* This also includes the Gentiles. Jesus Christ is Lord of all people. Now the church can be set free from its narrow minded thinking to witness across the border and around the world. Let them know that this Jesus Christ, by whom peace is made between God and man, is Lord of all; not only as over all, God blessed for evermore.

When Peter finally met with Cornelius, his family and friends (Acts 10:24-33), he spoke on the most crucial issue for himself and the Jewish Christians in general: *Ye know how that it is an unlawful thing for a man that is a Jew to keep company, or come unto one of another nation; but God hath shewed me that I should not call any man common or unclean* Acts 10:28. Peter was starting to understand what his vision truly means. God was tearing down his barrier of ethnic religious prejudice and ethnic pride, at least to the point of associating with Gentiles. Peter acknowledges that those Gentiles who fear God and do what is right are acceptable. In a sense, Peter was not ready to cross the border so he attempts to include those in the border that fear God in a broader definition of what constitutes God's people.

The fixed rule of judgment from the beginning during the time of Cain and Abel's offerings unto the Lord was: *If thou doest well, shalt thou not be accepted? And, if not well, sin,* and the punishment of it, *lie at the door,* Genesis. 4:7. This was always a truth, before Peter perceived it, *that God respecteth no man's person.* God does not care what country you are from, but what you did, how it affected Him and the persons around you and if your personal character received neither advantage nor disadvantage from the great difference that existed between Jews and Gentiles. It was clear that a great truth had been darkened by the covenant of peculiarity made with Israel, and the badges of distinction put upon them; the ceremonial law was a wall of partition between them and other nations; it is true that in it *God favoured that nation* Rom. 3:1, 2; 9:4. Some of the persons among them inferred that they were sure of God's acceptance, even though they lived as they listed, and that no Gentile could possibly be accepted of God. God had placed both Jew and Gentile on the same level by effectually abolishing the covenant of peculiarity, repealing the ceremonial law, and setting the matter at large by speaking through the prophets to prevent and rectify this mistake. Now, Peter was made to perceive it, by comparing the vision that he had with that which Cornelius had.

CHAPTER 3

Praise is What I Do

What is it about praise that you should be doing at all times? Praise is what gets God's attention when you want Him to hear your cry or plea.

Psalm 100
1 Make a joyful noise unto the LORD, all ye lands.
2 Serve the LORD with gladness: come before his presence with singing.
3 Know ye that the LORD he is God: it is he that hath made us, and not we ourselves; we are his people, and the sheep of his pasture.
4 Enter into his gates with thanksgiving, and into his courts with praise: be thankful unto him, and bless his name.
5 For the LORD is good; his mercy is everlasting; and his truth endureth to all generations.

The word praise actually means *thanksgiving* or, more specifically, *thank-offering*. It was one psalm that accompanied a "thank-offering" (Leviticus 7:11-21 *peace offering*) that one presented when God had especially answered a prayer or given a great deliverance. This psalm contains a command to serve (vv. 1-3) and a command to praise (vv. 4-5). Each section is in turn divided into three calls and three causes.

There are three calls to serve:

Make a joyful noise (v. 1) - You should be making a joyful noise unto Him for all that He has done for you.

Serve the Lord and **come before** (v. 2) – This is where you ought to be glad to come into the house of the Lord and serve Him with gladness. When we serve others we also serve God. You should be supporting, encouraging and uplifting one another because we need each other.

There are three causes for serving:

The Lord He is God, it is He that hath made us, and **we are His people** (v. 3) – You are a product of the Most High God because you did not create yourselves. He is your creator. Too many of you are living as though you are your own creator and center of your own little world. This is the type of mind set that leads you to having PRIDE, GREED, IDOLATRY and a loss of HOPE issues. What you are going through, he has already gone through because He was hated on, ridiculed and talked about. You were important to Him before you were important to yourselves. You must realize that God is your Creator and gives you all that you have. When God gives you all that you need you will want to give to others as God gave to you 2 Corinthians 9:8. What David is telling you is that you must acknowledge that the Lord is God and you do this when you shout your praises and appreciate Him as your Creator. You must accept His authority in every detail of your life and enthusiastically agree with the guidance He gives you. Express your thanks for His unfailing LOVE.

There are three calls to praise:

Enter into His gates with thanksgiving, be thankful and **bless His name** (v. 4) – God alone is worthy of being praised. Are you just going through the motions of reluctantly going to church Sunday after Sunday when you should be willingly and joyfully coming into the presence of the Most High God? You should walk into His presence with a praise in your mouth and a worship in your heart as you remember God's goodness and dependability so you can bless His wholly name.

There are three causes for praise:

The Lord is good, His mercy is everlasting and **His truth endureth to all generations** (v. 5) – God continues to pour out His mercy on you daily. His word says "Taste and see that the Lord is good" (Psalm 38:4). As we taste and see God's goodness we make discoveries and have enjoyment that is everlasting. Through trying and experience we learn that the Lord is good. As you taste and see, you take notice of it, and take the comfort of it.

You must take time to praise God because you do not know what is going to happen throughout your day but the Holy Spirit has your best interest at heart. One of your main responses to God is praise. Praise can never get you where worship can take you but it will take you to a place where you are getting ready for worship. You must open your mouth to give true praise unto God (Proverbs 27:21).

You should start your day from the time you wake up in the morning by giving Honor, Praise and Glory unto the Most High God because it was no effort of your own that you awoke this morning. What is it throughout your day that you love the most because you had nothing to do with the day being made. God made it and provided for you on this day. You should be rejoicing and glad that He has made it for you no matter what our situations and circumstances are. (Psalm 118:24). He is your God waiting up all night and day for you to cry out to Him so He could help you with any problem you may have. You must exalt Him and give thanks unto Him because you are His sons and daughters (Psalm 118:28).

Psalm 111
[1] Praise ye the Lord. I will praise the Lord with my whole heart, in the assembly of the upright, and in the congregation.
[2] The works of the Lord are great, sought out of all them that have pleasure therein.
[3] His work is honourable and glorious: and his righteousness endureth forever.
[4] He hath made his wonderful works to be remembered: the Lord is gracious and full of compassion.

⁵ He hath given meat unto them that fear him: he will ever be mindful of his covenant.

⁶ He hath shewed his people the power of his works, that he may give them the heritage of the heathen.

⁷ The works of his hands are verity and judgment; all his commandments are sure.

⁸ They stand fast for ever and ever, and are done in truth and uprightness.

⁹ He sent redemption unto his people: he hath commanded his covenant forever: holy and reverend is his name.

¹⁰ The fear of the LORD is the beginning of wisdom: a good understanding have all they that do his commandments: his praise endureth forever.

Verse 1 suggests that as you sing to the praise and glory of God," the heart, and the whole heart, without division and distraction, must be employed in the work. This kind of praise must not be in secret with just those that are in the council of the upright and the assembly of the righteous but also with those that are in public setting of worship. Praises unto God are to be shared with all men, women and children.

Verse 10 The word "beginning" in Scripture sometimes means the chief; and true religion is at once the first element of wisdom, and its chief fruit. To know God so as to walk aright before him is the greatest of all the applied sciences. Holy reverence of God leads us to praise him, and this is the point which the psalm drives at, for it is a wise act on the part of a creature towards his Creator. Obedience to God proves that our judgment is sound. Why should he not be obeyed?

Only a man void of understanding will ever justify rebellion against the holy God. Men may know and be very orthodox, they may talk and be very eloquent, they may speculate and be very profound; but the best proof of their intelligence must be found in their actually doing the will of the Lord. The former part of the psalm taught us the doctrine of God's nature and character, by describing his works: the second part supplies the practical lesson by drawing the inference that to worship and obey him is the dictate of true wisdom. We joyfully own that it is so. His praise endureth forever. The praises of God will never cease, because his works will always excite adoration, and it will always be the wisdom of men to extol their glorious Lord. Some regard this sentence as referring to those who fear the Lord—their praise shall endure forever: and, indeed, it is true that those who lead obedient lives shall obtain honor of the Lord, and commendations which will abide forever.

Fear is the first ingredient in wisdom. If you do not fear God but calls yourself wise, then you are only pretending to be wise. Only those that fear the Lord will depart from evil. If you live in sin, you are not only unwise but you are saying that you do not fear God. Those that fear the Lord do the things connected with the fear of the Lord; that is, who obey God. As God is always the same, so there is, as derived from his being and perfections, always the same foundation for praise. That is, the foundation for his praise endures to all eternity; or, is unchangeable.

Psalm 118: ²⁴ *This is the day which the LORD hath made; we will rejoice and be glad in it.*

This is where you are giving your Creator, Lord and Saviour all the praise and glory because He has given you life once again to enjoy the beauty of His creation. You must remember that you had nothing to do with your awakening this morning and you owe everything to Him. Because of the victory that God has won on this day you will be able to turn a day of despair into a day of worship and victory before the Lord. The doctrine of the Christian Sabbath is the day that the Lord has set aside for you: *It is the day which the Lord has made*, has made remarkable, made holy, has distinguished from other days; he has made it for man: it is therefore called *the Lord's day*, for it bears his image and superscription. The duty of the Sabbath, the work of the day that is to be done in his day: *We will rejoice and be glad in it*, not only in the institution of the day, that there is such a day appointed, but in the occasion of it, Christ's becoming the *head of the corner*. This you ought to rejoice in both as his honor and your advantage. Sabbath days must be rejoicing days, and then they are to you as the days of heaven. See what a good Master you serve, who, having instituted a day for his service, appoints it to be spent in holy joy.

Psalm 118: [28] *Thou art my God, and I will praise thee: thou art my God, I will exalt thee.*

The psalmist wants you to praise God for yourself, and endeavour to exalt him in his own heart and in the hearts of others, and this because of his covenant-relation to him and interest in him: "*Thou art my God*, on whom you depend on for everything, and to whom you have devoted your life, who

CHAPTER 4

Spiritual Freedom

Galatians 5:1 Stand fast therefore in the liberty wherewith Christ hath made us free, and be not entangled again with the yoke of bondage.

The liberty that is spoken of here is a right in which a person has to act, that we may do or forbear the doing of things at our pleasure, as we apprehend them suitable or not, without the delay or hindrance of anyone else. The liberty here, is that freedom from the Law, from the curse of the moral law, and from the co-action of it, and principally from the ceremonial law contained in ordinances. This is the liberty that Christ has purchased for us, and in which the Apostle Paul wills for all believers to stand fast; not being again entangled with a yoke, which God had taken off our necks. *Come unto me, all ye that labour and are heavy laden, and I will give you rest. Take my yoke upon you, and learn of me; for I am meek and lowly in heart: and ye shall find rest unto your souls. For my yoke is easy, and my burden is light.* Matthew 11:28-30. The disciples, in their assembly or meeting, had called it a yoke. *And put no difference between us and them, purifying their hearts by faith. Now therefore why tempt ye God, to put a yoke upon the neck of the disciples, which neither our fathers nor we were able to bear? But we believe that through the grace of the* LORD *Jesus Christ we shall be saved, even as they* Acts 15:9-11. The Law was given to Israelites, not to justify them, but to restrain them from transgressions, and by making them sensible of their sins and to lead them to Christ for justification.

The words *"stand fast"* is an expression of the Greek word *"STEKOS"*, which means *"to stand firm, persevere, to hold one's ground"*. **We must stand fast in protecting our Spiritual Freedom.** Apostle Paul reveals that our freedom in Christ does not just come automatically. There is a part that we must play in getting that Spiritual Freedom. Satan, is always seeking whom he may devour. *Be sober, be vigilant; because your adversary the devil, as a roaring lion, walketh about, seeking whom he may devour:* 1 Peter 5:8. We must make every effort to resist every attempt that Satan uses to draw us back into self-effort. One of Satan's greatest weapons is, legalism; which is getting us to adhere to a literal interpretation of a law, rule, or religious or moral code. When Paul compared being under the Law to being a descendant of the slave woman, Hagar, we need to be steadfast in defending our liberty that we have received through faith in Christ because none of us want to be cast out from the inheritance of God. *Tell me, ye that desire to be under the law, do ye not hear the law? For it is written,* *that Abraham had two sons, the one by a bondmaid, the other by a freewoman. But he who was of the bondwoman was born after the flesh; but he of the freewoman was by promise* Galatians 4:21-23. Now, in this liberty, the children of the free woman, believers under the Gospel dispensation, are very pertinently exhorted to stand fast, in consequence and consideration of their character; that is we should highly prize it, as man does their civil liberty to maintain and defend it at all costs. We should abide by the doctrine of it without wavering, and without fear; keep up the practice of it, by obeying with the whole heart the doctrine of it, by becoming the servants of righteousness, by frequent attendance at the throne of Grace, and continual observance of the ordinances of Christ. This liberty could not in any of its branches be obtained by us, by any merit, by any righteousness, by any act of ours, but is wholly of Christ's procuring for us, both by power and price, whereby He was ransomed and delivered us out of the hands of all our spiritual enemies; sin, Satan, the Law, and death.

"Liberty" means, the condition of being free from restrictions or control and being physically and legally free from confinement, servitude, or forced labor. The liberty that Paul is speaking of is specifically the freedom from the oppression of the Old Testament Law; *Now we know that what things soever the law saith, it saith to them who are under the law: that every mouth may be stopped, and all the world may become guilty before God.* Romans 3:19 Paul made it clear that this liberty is not freedom to sin but freedom from sin. If we use our freedom in Christ to indulge our sinful passions, we will pay a price; *For, brethren, ye have been called unto liberty; only*

use not liberty for an occasion to the flesh, but by love serve one another. Galatians 5:13 Paul was not out of control because he was controlled by his love for the Lord instead of his fear of punishment for breaking the Old Testament Law.

What Liberty does Paul mean?

This is either in things of a civil nature, or of a spiritual nature. It is not of the civil nature (this is the government's department), because it is not of the liberty that Christ has made us free. Civil liberty will give children freedom from the laws of their parents or give servants freedom from the commands of their masters. In today's world when the people obey neither the laws of God nor the laws of men is called carnal liberty. The liberty that Paul is speaking of is far better than both, carnal and civil. It is the liberty "wherewith Christ has made us free", not from material bonds but free from the eternal wrath of God.

Where is this liberty? In our conscience

Our conscience is free and quiet because it no longer has to fear the wrath of God. God will never be angry with us because of the price Christ paid for us and will forever be merciful to us. It is marvelous indeed to have God as our friend and Father who will defend, sustain, and save us in the life and the life to come. Since the wrath of God has been satisfied by Christ we are free from the Law, sin, death, Satan, hell, etc. Not one of these foes can condemn and accuse us anymore. But yet they will try to separate us from the love of God. *For I am persuaded, that neither death, nor life, nor angels, nor principalities, nor powers, nor things present, nor things to come, Nor height, nor depth, nor any other creature, shall be able to separate us from the love of God, which is in Christ Jesus our Lord* Romans 8:38-39. If we train our conscience to think on the freedom that was purchased for us by Christ then the fears of the Law, the terrors of sin, the horror of death that attacks us occasionally shall not endure. *In a little wrath I hid my face from thee for a moment; but with everlasting kindness will I have mercy on thee, saith the* LORD *thy Redeemer. For this is as the waters of Noah unto me: for as I have sworn that the waters of Noah should no more go over the earth; so have I sworn that I would not be wroth with thee, nor rebuke thee* Isaiah 54:8-9. This liberty that Christ, the Son of God purchased with His own blood was not given to us by the Law, or for our own righteousness but given to us freely for Christ's sake. *If the Son therefore shall make you free, ye shall be free indeed* John 8:36.

When we are "entangled" in something, we are entwined, twisted together, snarled; to complicate; confuse. The Galatians were so entwined in the Old Testament Laws that, the demands in which they were trying to find God's favor or acceptance through performance had placed them in bondage. Christ paid the ultimate price for our liberty. Freedom from self-justification through the law was purchased by Christ upon the cross. We must never let anything or anyone bring us back into bondage again. Now that freedom has been given to us by Christ, that freedom is our goal and our responsibility.

What Paul means by *"the yoke of bondage"* is the Law that the Jews called "the yoke of the commandments"; particularly the ceremonial law, as circumcision, which Peter represents as a yoke intolerable: *And put no difference between us and them, purifying their hearts by faith. Now therefore why tempt ye God, to put a yoke upon the neck of the disciples, which neither our fathers nor we were able to bear? But we believe that through the grace of the* LORD *Jesus Christ we shall be saved, even as they* Acts 15:9-11. Every doctrine and ordinance of man is a yoke of bondage which should not be submitted to. Any action whatsoever performed in a religious way and in order for a man's acceptance with God, and to obtain his favour, and according to his observance of which He judges of his state, and speaks peace and comfort to himself, is a yoke of bondage.

We must stand fast therefore in the liberty that we have from Abraham's justification by faith that proved, who so ever believe in Christ, and the promises of God through Him are the seed of Abraham. Paul, exhorts the Galatian believers to stand fast in the freedom from the Mosaic Law which had been obtained for them by Christ, and was announced to them by the gospel and not to be held fast in the yoke of bondage as if it was necessary for Salvation.

All true Christians *(those that trust, live, and honour the word of God)*, that are being taught by the Holy Spirit will wait for eternal life, which is the reward of righteousness and the object of their hope, as their gift from God because of their faith in Jesus Christ and not because of their own works. True faith is a working grace, it works by our love to God and to our fellow Christians because God is love. Without faith working by love, all else is worthless. Will we be among those who, take heed to the warnings that Apostle Paul talks about in being steadfast in the word of God and in the liberty of the Gospel. Jesus Christ will not own up to any one as their Saviour who will not rely upon Him as their only Saviour. What apostle Paul was trying to accomplish by bringing forward threats and promises to the Galatians was so that they will give up the extremely wicked or villainous doctrine of the false apostles to keep them in the liberty that Christ purchased for them. It is of Paul's proclaiming in the Gospel, and of his applying it by his Spirit, whom the Lord sends down into our hearts as a free Spirit, to get us acquainted with it, who works faith in us to lay hold upon us so that we may receive this blessing of Grace and be not entangled again with the yoke of bondage.

We are to be firm and unwavering in maintaining the great principles of our Christian liberty. We have been freed from the bondage of rites and ceremonies; and we should not by any means, and in no form, yield to them again. The Jewish convert might observe the ceremonies or assert their liberty, the Gentile might disregard them or might attend them, provided he did not depend upon them. We must not again allow such a yoke to be put upon us; we must not become slaves to any rites, rituals, customs and habits. God promised to justify by faith, Abraham in the covenant. The Law of Moses that was given long after this covenant, could neither annul nor alter this covenant, by introducing a method of justification different from that which was so solemnly established thereby.

Think of it like this, imagine that you were in prison for 1, 2, 3 or even 5 years but had a sentence of 15 to 20 years and then suddenly you find out that you have been pardoned and set free. You had nothing to do with this because all your parole hearings were denied. You were not even aware how and when it happened but there you are standing outside the prison walls a free man. It is now your responsibility to live as a free person. Paul's letter to the Galatians talked about all being condemned prisoners of the Law and doomed to live under its severe restrictions because all the Law could do is point out our transgressions, *Wherefore then serveth the law? It was added because of transgressions, till the seed should come to whom the promise was made; and it was ordained by angels in the hand of a mediator* Galatians 3:19 all being a prisoner of sin, *But the scripture hath concluded all under sin, that the promise by faith of Jesus Christ might be given to them that believe* Galatians 3:22 locked up and prisoners of the Law, *But before faith came, we were kept under the law, shut up unto the faith which should afterwards be revealed* Galatians 3:23 we were in slavery under the basic principles of the world, *Even so we, when we were children, were in bondage under the elements of the world:* Galatians 4:3. Our release from prison and our release from slavery was given because Jesus Christ, *Who gave himself for our sins, that he might deliver us from this present evil world, according to the will of God and our Father:* Galatians 1:4. So the nature of our freedom is clear. We have been delivered from the judgment of the Law of God, and we no longer live under its disciplinary regulations.

CHAPTER 5

Power to Do Above and Beyond

Ephesians 3:20 Now unto him that is able to do exceeding abundantly above all that we ask or think, according to the power that worketh in us,

We all have our own prayers that we pray to the Lord. During our prayer time we sometimes cry, weep and ask the Lord for certain things. Sometimes we seek the Lord for protection from unknown and sometimes known dangers. We also use our prayer time for looking back and seeing what God has done and we delight to see His marvelous works He has done in us and through us. There comes a time when we have heard enough of the testimonies about what God has done for someone else and about His glory in Christ. When we reach this point we should have a worship in our hearts and a praise in our mouths that we want to shout choruses of Hallelujah exalting His greatness. This is exactly how Paul felt when he said the prayer in verses 14-19. Paul wanted us to be so moved by the truth that he spoken in the prior chapters so that our focus would not, cannot and should not dare rest on ourselves but on Him, our Lord, our glorious King and Majestic Lover.

It was not uncommon for Paul to utter a praise, to Him from whom all blessings come and to whom all thanks is due, in the midst of an argument. *For of him, and through him, and to him, are all things: to whom be glory for ever. Amen.* Romans 11:36 When Paul finished his energetic prayer in verses 14-19 he went into a doxology (A hymn, prayer, or formula of worship in praise of God), literally a "word of glory" (Greek *doxa* - "glory," *logos* - "word"). Doxologies are short, spontaneous ascriptions of praise to God, usually having three parts: 1. The one to whom glory is given, 2. The ascription of glory, and 3. The expression "forever and ever". Paul's doxology was adapted to strengthen our faith. He was strengthening our faith so that we did not struggle in believing that what we asked God for was not too much for Him to give or too much for us to expect from Him. Even after He has given us exceeding and abundant blessings we were able to ask for more. He not only will give to us after He has done abundantly but He will give us above all that we could either think or ask. God is able to establish you to the end, and do all for you that has been desired according to the power of the indwelling Holy Spirit that worketh in us and appeals to our experience; *Likewise the Spirit also helpeth our infirmities: for we know not what we should pray for as we ought: but the Spirit itself maketh intercession for us with groanings which cannot be uttered;* Romans 8:26. The things Paul prayed for in verses

14-19 (spiritual strength, the indwelling Jesus, experiential knowledge of God's love, and the fullness of God) belong to us as children of God. However, they must be received by believing prayer and can be furthered in the lives of others by our prayers for them. God is the object of Paul's doxology, *"Him who is able,"* infinitely able! He is described as the one whose power is unlimited in His people.

Paul was praising God for 2 things: His amazing Power and His amazing Glory. The exceeding greatness of His Power, whereby God works faith and preserve to salvation, and enables us to bear our afflictions. *Be not thou therefore ashamed of the testimony of our Lord, nor of me his prisoner: but be thou partaker of the afflictions of the gospel according to the power of God;* 2 Timothy 1:8 We shall experience a change not only in our view of things, but in our hearts, our dispositions, our words and actions, and in all the powers of our souls, through the mighty working of the power of God in us. Now our faith is sufficient to receive all the blessings promised to us through the word of God, particularly the blessing of a complete restoration to the conformity of the image of God's son; *And we know that all things work together for good to them that love God, to them who are the called according to his purpose.* Romans 8:28, *Herein is our love made perfect, that we may have boldness in the day of judgment: because as he is, so are we in this world.* 1 John 4:17, in this life and happiness greater that we can ever imagine in the life to come.

Paul still was not satisfied, even though his prayer had reached beyond which neither faith, nor hope, nor imagination could go. Paul had broken out into thanksgiving, which serves the additional purpose of exhorting the Ephesians to maintain good hope through grace, *Now our Lord Jesus Christ himself, and God, even our Father, which hath loved us, and hath given us everlasting consolation and good hope through grace,* 2 Thessalonians 2:16, and to constantly obtain more and more adequate conceptions of the value of the grace of God. We cannot offer to God proper or sincere thanksgiving for favors received. Having exhausted all the forms of prayer, Paul casts himself on the infinitude - the state or quality of being infinite or having no limit of God, in full confidence that God can and will do all that is according to His will. God's power, not our prayers nor what we think is the measure of Paul's anticipations and desires. God is not only unlimited in Himself, but is unrestricted by our prayers or knowledge. The infinite power of God from which so much may be expected, is the same of which we are now subjects, according to what we feel within ourselves. Every benefit which God bestows upon us is a manifestation of His grace, and love, and power, in consequence of which we ought to cherish a stronger confidence for the future. The past is a foretale and pledge of the future. Those who have been raised from the dead, who have been transformed by the renewing of their minds, *And be not conformed to this world: but be ye transformed by the renewing of your mind, that ye may prove what is that good, and acceptable, and perfect, will of God* Romans 12:2, translated from the kingdom of darkness into the kingdom of God's dear Son, and in whom God Himself dwells by His Spirit, having already experienced a change which nothing but God could effect, may well join in the doxology to *Him who is able to do exceeding abundantly above all we can ask or think.*

And Solomon said, Thou hast shewed unto thy servant David my father great mercy, according as he walked before thee in truth, and in righteousness, and in uprightness of heart with thee; and thou hast kept for him this great kindness, that thou hast given him a son to sit on his throne, as it is this day. And now, O Lord my God, thou hast made thy servant king instead of David my father: and I am but a little child: I know not how to go out or come in. And thy servant is in the midst of thy people which thou hast chosen, a great people, that cannot be numbered nor counted for multitude. Give therefore thy servant an understanding heart to judge thy people, that I may discern between good and bad: for who is able to judge this thy so great a people? And the speech pleased the Lord, that Solomon had asked this thing. And God said unto him, Because thou hast asked this thing, and hast not asked for thyself long life; neither hast asked riches for thyself, nor hast asked the life of thine enemies; but hast asked for thyself understanding to discern judgment; Behold, I have done according to thy words: lo, I have given thee a wise and an understanding heart; so that there was none like thee before thee, neither after thee shall any arise like unto thee. And I have also given thee that which thou hast not asked, both riches, and honour: so that there shall not be any among the kings like unto thee all thy days. And if thou wilt walk in my ways, to keep my statutes and my commandments, as thy father David did walk, then I will lengthen thy days.
1 Kings 3:6-14

God is able to do more than any man can ask for, just as He did for Solomon. God knows what we want and what we need before we ask, and He has already made provisions for His people before we ask for anything. Some of the things that He has provided for us, we never could and others we never should have asked for, had He not provided them for us. If not for the indwelling Holy Spirit in us, we would not know what to ask for. Because of the indwelling Spirit, meaning the Spirit of God, who is the finger and Power of God, who begins and carries on, and will finish the work of grace in us, and which is an evidence of the exceeding greatness of the Power of God that we should be proclaiming to the world, we are able to ask God for the things we need and then some.

Who is able to do exceeding abundantly? God, because He is omnipotent, is able to do all things and is able to do supernaturally above the greatest abundance. We can ask for every good thing that we have heard of or every good that God has promised in His word. *And we know that all things work together for good to them that love God, to them who are the called according to his purpose,* Romans 8:28. After all, God is able to do more for us than we can ask or think and His ability here is so necessarily connected with His willingness, that the one indisputably implies the other. All that God has promised to do and all that He can do and all that will be done according to what He has done, by the power of the Holy Spirit, which worketh in us. This power acts with energy in our hearts, expels evil, purify and refine our affections and desires while implanting good. The limiting factor is not what we can ask or imagine. The limiting factor is the power *(dunamis)* that is working *(energeo)* in us. Whose power? God's power! There is no limit to God's power. Paul has been praying and instructing us in prayer. He is brimming to the top and running over with an awareness of the limitless power of God at work in us. And we worry about asking things of God that are too big. Shame on us! Our ability to "ask or imagine" may be limited, but not God's power.

God can and does work beyond our ability to ask. When you go in for an operation, you don't need to understand all the technology that will be used by the surgeon and the surgeon's team. You just have to believe they can get the job done and ask for the operation. It's their job to know more than you.

The God Paul serves is huge in his mind and faith. Nothing is too great to ask of Him.

CHAPTER 6

Suit Up for Battle

Ephesians 6:11-12 Put on the whole armour of God, that ye may be able to stand against the wiles of the devil. For we wrestle not against flesh and blood, but against principalities, against powers, against the rulers of the darkness of this world, against spiritual wickedness in high places.

Are you battle ready? At some point in our lives we will be called into Spiritual warfare. We must learn how to fight in a way that honors and depends upon God. If you are walking with God in you and have allowed the Holy Spirit to guide and direct your life then you are ready. If you are walking by the flesh and have not let the Holy Spirit in your heart then you not ready. The Lord prepares us for the battles He knows that we can fight. He prepares you by the renewing of your mind *And be not conformed to this world: but be ye transformed by the renewing of your mind, that ye may prove what is that good, and acceptable, and perfect, will of God.* Romans 12:2 and the cleansing of your heart *Create in me a clean heart, O God; and renew a right spirit within me.* Psalms 51:10

We as Christians are engaged in a battle from now on until the Lord's return. There is no time-out, no temporary truce or even a cease-fire. If you belong to the kingdom of God then you are a primary target for the attacks of the world, our own flesh and Satan. Resist him, and he will flee. If we give way, he will get ground. If we distrust either our cause, or our Leader, or our Spiritual armour, we give Satan an advantage. Thankfully, our King has not left us to fend off these attacks on our own. He has provided us the Holy Spirit to guide us into all truth and has given us the most powerful arsenal of weapons to mankind; the armour of God.

The Holy Spirit that lives in you that you have let take over you will prepare your heart and mind for battle because the battle you will fight is not against flesh and blood but against principalities. The combat is not against human enemies, nor against our own corrupt nature; we have to deal with an enemy who has a thousand ways of beguiling unstable souls. The devils assault us in the things that belong to our souls, and labour to deface the heavenly image in our hearts.

According to scripture, the Lord has already provided us with the protection and power we need to engage in battle and come out victorious. The Christian Spiritual armour is made to be worn; and there is no putting off our armour till we have done our warfare, and finished our course. Just as armour needs to be put on the body piece by piece to be effective, we must put on every one of these weapons of our warfare to be truly ready to use them. *For though we walk in the flesh, we do not war after the flesh: For the weapons of our warfare are not carnal, but mighty through God to the pulling down of strong holds; Casting down imaginations, and every high thing that exalteth itself against the knowledge of God, and bringing into captivity every thought to the obedience of Christ;* 2 Corinthians 10: 3-5 Let me ask you this, what is the most important thing you need in battle? That is why we must put on and keep on our Spiritual armour at all times. We cannot fight Spiritual attacks with fleshly weapons, we will definitely lose. The whole armour of God gives us the practical means to be mighty and victorious warriors by putting on Christ in all His fullness. *But put ye on the Lord Jesus Christ, and make not provision for the flesh, to fulfil the lusts thereof.* Romans 13:14

Repeat after me and say it with authority, I am battle ready, because God has given me the Holy Spirit and His Spiritual armour.

Before we put this armour on let me say this, as Jesus' disciples, we follow Him into the battle to take back what the kingdom of darkness has stolen- and to stand against the enemy's schemes to distract, deceive, and disarm God's people. *The thief cometh not, but for to steal, and to kill, and to destroy: I am come that they might have life, and that they might have it more abundantly.* John 10: 10

Ephesians 6: [14] Stand therefore, having your loins girt about with truth, and having on the breastplate of righteousness; [15] And your feet shod with the preparation of the gospel of peace; [16] Above all, taking the shield of faith, wherewith ye shall be able to quench all the fiery darts of the wicked. [17] And take the helmet of salvation, and the sword of the Spirit, which is the word of God:

The whole armour of God consists of six pieces. **The first is the Belt of Truth**. Now the soldier's "loins" or (**waist**) were girt about with a leather belt. The belt was crafted of tough leather strips and small brass plates for extra protection. Wrapped about the waist this leather belt clung closely to the soldier and shielded some of the most vulnerable areas of the body. When preparing for battle, a soldier would put on His belt first. The belt was designed to keep other pieces of his armour in place, including his sword. The soldier would also wear a tunic, which was a cloak worn over a short kilt or skirt. Prior to engaging in combat, the soldier would tuck his tunic under his belt, providing maximum movement of freedom for his legs.

v.14, TRUTH, it is the knowledge of the truth of God's word, *If so be that ye have heard him, and have been taught by him, as the truth is in Jesus:* Ephesians 4:21 To be girted with truth is to be firmly established in the truth of God's word. God's word is truth and is therefore foundational and all the other pieces of a Christian's spiritual armour depend on, and are held in place by our spiritual belt of truth. Jesus said, *Then said Jesus to those Jews which believed on him, If ye continue in* *my word, then are ye my disciples indeed;* ³² *And ye shall know the truth, and the truth shall make you free.* John 8:31 Just as the soldier's belt provided freedom of movement we are kept free from the enemy's lies by abiding in God's truth. Satan will attack our truth with lies because he is the Father of all lies. He attacks the promises of God just as he did in the Garden of Eden when he told Eve, *Now the serpent was more subtil than any beast of the field which the* LORD *God had made. And he said unto the woman, Yea, hath God said, Ye shall not eat of every tree of the garden? And the woman said unto the serpent, We may eat of the fruit of the trees of the garden: But of the fruit of the tree which is in the midst of the garden, God hath said, Ye shall not eat of it, neither shall ye touch it, lest ye die. And the serpent said unto the woman, Ye shall not surely die:* Genesis 3:1-4 If the enemy can get you to doubt God's integrity then you will end up in a downward spiral because one lie leads to another and then another until you are utterly discouraged, confused and defeated. But don't fall for it! Open your heart to the searchlight of God's word and allow the Holy Spirit to guide you into all truth. *Howbeit when he, the Spirit of truth, is come, he will guide you into all truth: for he shall not speak of himself; but whatsoever he shall hear, that shall he speak: and he will shew you things to come* John 16:13

The second is the **breastplate of righteousness** which was a central part of the Roman soldier's armor—it provided protection for the torso, which contains vital organs like the heart, lungs and so on. Without a breastplate, a soldier would be asking for death, as any attack could instantly become fatal. With a sturdy breastplate, the very same attacks become ineffective and useless, as blows glance off the armor.

v.14, the breastplate of righteousness; Putting on the armour of God involves guarding our vital spiritual organ (heart) above all else. *Keep thy heart with all diligence; for out of it are the issues of life* Proverbs 4:23 God wants your whole heart and nothing less, for a heart sets the course of a person's life because out of the abundance of the heart the mouth speaks. The heart is so important because *For with the heart man believeth unto righteousness; and with the mouth confession is made unto salvation* Romans 10:10 God offers us His righteousness on the basis of faith in His son. *Even the righteousness of God which is by faith of Jesus Christ unto all and upon all them that believe: for there is no difference:* Romans 3:22 Without righteousness, we leave ourselves open to almost certain death. With righteousness—just as with a breastplate—the otherwise fatal attacks of our enemy are thwarted. It is not our own goodness that protects our hearts because all our righteousness is as a filthy rag (Isaiah 64:6). But God protects those that are clothed in His righteousness. *No weapon that is formed against thee shall prosper; and every tongue that shall rise against thee in judgment thou shalt condemn. This is the heritage of the servants of the* LORD, *and their righteousness is of me, saith the* LORD. Isaiah 54:17 Whenever the enemy tries to bring up your past, the breastplate of righteousness is your defense. If the Spirit of Christ dwells in you, then your heavenly Father receives you as His son or daughter no matter what the devil says. *For he hath made him to be sin for us, who knew no sin; that we might be made the righteousness of God in* *him.* 2 Corinthians 5:21 The righteousness of Christ in you is all that matters and not your past or failures.

The third is, **preparation of the gospel of peace**, no soldier can go far without the proper shoes. Even with all his other weapons, a barefoot soldier would soon become immobilized by the rough terrain taking its toll on his feet. A roman soldier's caligae or sandals were constructed of leather and laced up the center of the foot and onto the ankle. The design of the shoe may look like it does not give much protection to the soldier's feet but the sandals were very functional. The openness of the sandals enabled the soldier to wear them all day in his work, in marching, in fighting and in standing for a long period of time without getting blisters. The thick soles of the sandals were studded through with iron hobnails. These provided good traction and also came in handy when trampling the enemy.

v. 15, preparation of the gospel of peace, or shoes of peace. As the Roman soldiers wore special shoes called caligae on his feet, enabling him to advance against his enemy, so the Christian must have on his feet a sense of eagerness or willingness to advance against the devil and take the fight to him. Such eagerness to contend with Satan comes from the gospel of peace. The gospel gives peace to the believer although he advances against such a powerful opponent. As Paul told Timothy, *Preach the word; be instant in season, out of season; reprove, rebuke, exhort with all long suffering and doctrine.* 2 Timothy 4:2 We must be ready at all times and in the army of God there is time for rest and refreshment but there is never a time for complacency. Any Christian who let their guard down and get comfortable during a temporary cease-fire will not be ready when their enemies come in for the kill. When you are equipped with the gospel of peace your enemy has no chance at getting to you. *When the wicked, even mine enemies and my foes, came upon me to eat up my flesh, they stumbled and fell.* Psalms 27:2 When Jesus was tempted by the devil, the devil left him for a season *And when the devil had ended all the temptation, he departed from him for a season* Luke 4:13. No doubt the devil would be back; *But when he had turned about and looked on his disciples, he rebuked Peter, saying, Get thee behind me, Satan: for thou savourest not the things that be of God, but the things that be of men.* Mark 8:33

The fourth is, **the shield of Faith**, the Roman shield was made from bonded wood strips and covered in leather. The shield was not flat but semicircular so that anything that was thrown at the soldier would be deflected to one side. Iron or brass rims were fitted along the edges of the shield, and a leather strap was fastened to the back. The shield had a metal projection in the center which was used to stun or wind the opponent, easing the soldier's subsequent strike with his sword. Before the Romans went into battle they would soak their shields in water to deter the opponent's fiery arrows from catching their shield on fire. Also, they did a maneuver called the tortoise where the frontline soldiers would place their shields in front of them side by side and the ones in the middle would balance theirs on their helmets. As long as the soldiers held this formation, the enemy would have trouble defeating them.

v. 16, shield of faith; means taking God at His word by believing His promises without seeing the visible evidence. *Now faith is the substance of things hoped for, the evidence of things not seen.* Hebrews 11:1 This trust will protect you from doubts that Satan will try to plant in you. Thus, wielding the shield of faith involves holding fast to the word of the Lord and watching the Lord defend and fight for us. *Every word of God is pure: he is a shield unto them that put their trust in him.* Proverbs 30:5; *As for God, his way is perfect; the word of the LORD is tried: he is a buckler to all them that trust in him.* 2 Samuel 22:31 Each of us will face difficult situations and temptations of the enemy at one time or another. But you see that shield of faith is the protection that God has provided for us to get through these tests. In temptation, the devil will try to get us to believe the lie that sin can provide a better life than God can. Our shield of faith will deflect that attack with the belief that God is providing us with all we need. In a difficult situation, the devil will try to use fear to get our eyes off Jesus. *Looking unto Jesus the author and finisher of our faith;* Hebrews 12:2 Our shield of faith will deflect that attack with the belief that nothing is too hard for the Lord. *Behold, I am the LORD, the God of all flesh: is there any thing too hard for me?* Jeremiah 32:27 If the devil can get us to doubt God, he has temporary victory in our lives, *And he that doubteth is damned if he eat, because he eateth not of faith:* **for whatsoever is not of faith is sin.** Romans 14:23 However, when the devil is faced with authentic faith, the powers of darkness will be overcome. John said in *For whatsoever is born of God overcometh the world: and this is the victory that overcometh the world, even our faith.* 1 John 5:4

The fifth is, **the Helmet of Salvation**; A Roman soldier's helmet protected their skull and neck from the enemy's blows and falling debris. The helmet was made from bronze or iron; it included two hinged side pieces to protect the cheekbones and jaw. The helmets were often lined inside with sponge or felt for comfort. Horsehair plumes frequently adorned the tops of the soldier's helmets. Although, not used in battle, these plumes were dyed a variety of colors to distinguish the rank of military officers and were primarily used for ceremonial purposes.

v. 17, the helmet of salvation; Just as the breastplate of righteousness was adorned to protect the heart, the helmet of salvation is worn to protect the mind. Paul described this helmet as the "the hope of salvation" in *But let us, who are of the day, be sober, putting on the breastplate of faith and love; and for an helmet, the hope of salvation.* 1 Thessalonians 5:8 This is the assurance (certainty) of salvation. The helmet of salvation protects a Christian's mind by providing hope, which is a joyful and confident expectation that God will keep His promises. *For we are saved by hope: but hope that is seen is not hope: for what a man seeth, why doth he yet hope for? ²⁵ But if we hope for that we see not, then do we with patience wait for it.* Romans 8:24 Anyone without hope is vulnerable to the enemy's lies that life is not worth living. Many of Satan's battle against us happen in the mind. The devil can flash lewd and evil thoughts in our minds, hoping that we will entertain his thoughts and commit sin. *Let no man say when he is tempted, I am tempted of God: for God cannot be tempted with evil, neither tempteth he any man: But every man* *is tempted, when he is drawn away of his own lust, and enticed. Then when lust hath conceived, it bringeth forth sin: and sin, when it is finished, bringeth forth death.* James 1:13-15

The sixth is, **the Sword of the Spirit, which is the Word of God**; the Roman sword was crafted of iron. Blacksmiths hardened the iron by coating the red-hot sword blade with coal dust, thus forming a hard carbon coating on the blade. Sword handles were made of iron, ivory, bone, or wood. The Romans used their swords both offensively and defensively. Used in a defensive manner, the sword, along with the other armor pieces, enabled the soldier to deflect the enemy's blows. As an offensive weapon, the sword was used to attack and counter-attack an enemy until the weapon seriously wounded or killed the assailant. In battle, rows of Roman soldiers pressed back their enemies one step at a time by alternating a forward thrust of the shield with a forward thrust of the sword.

v. 17, the sword of the spirit, which is the word of God; Paul described Jesus as having a tongue with a two-edged sword in *And he had in his right hand seven stars: and out of his mouth went a sharp twoedged sword: and his countenance was as the sun shineth in his strength.* Revelation 1:16 God's word, which is our sword of the spirit, is able to cut down the strongholds of Satan. Too often we as Christians fail to use our swords but will display them as decorative pieces, beautiful to look at but of little practical use. *Let the high praises of God be in their mouth, and a two-edged sword in their hand;* Psalms 149:6 that double-edged sword is the word of God, and it is a powerful spiritual weapon, perfectly suited for spiritual battles. *For* *the word of God is quick, and powerful, and sharper than any twoedged sword, piercing even to the dividing asunder of soul and spirit, and of the joints and marrow, and is a discerner of the thoughts and intents of the heart.* Hebrews 4:12

Now that we are suited and booted for this spiritual battle now what? Well, let's look at verse 18.

Praying always with all prayer and supplication in the Spirit, and watching thereunto with all perseverance and supplication for all saints; Ephesians 6:18

The word **praying** can be linked to "stand" in v. 14 because without prayer God's armor is inadequate or useless to achieve our victory over Satan and the enemy. Prayer is indispensable. **Always** means on every occasion when Satan attacks. **In the Spirit** signifies that with the Spirit's help our prayer for divine aid will be made. **Watching thereunto** means being vigilant in this very matter of prayer. We are not to pray just for ourselves but also **for all saints**, spiritual combat is both an individual and corporate matter.

This is one of the prayers that I pray in the morning before I leave for work.
Full Armor of God Prayer

Lord, help me to put on the full spiritual armor You have provided for me so that I can "stand against the wiles of the devil" every day and show me how to gird up the core of my being with Your truth so I don't fall into deception of any kind. Teach me to not only know Your truth, but to live in it.

Lord, help me to put on the breastplate of righteousness that protects me from the enemy's attacks. I know it is Your righteousness in me that protects me, but I also know I must not neglect to put on Your righteousness like a bulletproof vest by doing what is right in Your eyes. Reveal to me thoughts, attitudes, and habits of my heart that are not pleasing to You. Show me what I have done, or am about to do, that does not glorify You. I want to see anything in me that violates Your high standards for my life so I can confess it, turn away from it, and be cleansed from all unrighteousness.

Thank You, Jesus, that I have peace beyond comprehension because of what You accomplished on the cross for me. Help me to stand secure with my feet protected by the good news that You have already prepared and secured for me. Because I have peace with You and from You, I am able to not only stand strong but to walk forward against the enemy and take back territory he has stolen from us all.

Lord, thank You that You have given me faith and have grown my faith in Your Word. I don't have faith in my own faith, as if I have accomplished anything myself, but I have faith in You and Your faithfulness to me, which is a shield from the enemy's arrows. Just as You were Abraham's shield and David's shield, You are mine as well. Thank You that even if my faith is shaky one day, Your faithfulness never is. Help me to remember Your faithfulness at all times. Enable me to take up the shield of faith as constant protection from the enemy.

Lord, help me to put on the helmet of salvation to protect my head and mind each day by remembering all You have saved me from, including the lies of the enemy. Enable me to remember only what You say about me and not what the enemy wants me to believe. Thank You that Your helmet of salvation protects me from warfare in my mind. Your salvation gives me everything I need in order to live successfully.

Lord, help me to take up the sword of the Spirit every day, for Your Word not only protects me from the enemy, but it is my greatest weapon against him. Enable me to always pray as Your Spirit leads me, and to keep on praying as long as I should. Teach me to be the strong and unshakable prayer warrior You want me to be so I can accomplish Your will.

Lord, this I pray in the name of Your precious Son, Jesus Christ, Amen.

CHAPTER 7

Plans to Prosper You

Jeremiah 29: [11] For I know the thoughts that I think toward you, saith the LORD, thoughts of peace, and not of evil, to give you an expected end.

This verse came in the middle of God's pronounced judgment of 70 years captivity for Judah by King Nebuchadnezzar, King of Babylon. The judgment of bondage started back in Jeremiah 25: [4] *And the LORD hath sent unto you all his servants the prophets, rising early and sending them; but ye have not hearkened, nor inclined your ear to hear.* After Jeremiah spoke desolation to the people of Judah, they tried to kill him but he escaped. As a symbol to God's judgment of bondage for Judah, Jeremiah puts a yoke on his neck; Thus *saith the LORD to me; Make thee bonds and yokes, and put them upon thy neck,* Jeremiah 27:2. The people of Judah did not like what Jeremiah was saying so they had their own prophets, diviners, dreamers, enchanter and sorcerers tell them lies concerning their captivity by Babylon. *Therefore hearken not unto the words of the prophets that speak unto you, saying, Ye shall not serve the king of Babylon: for they prophesy a lie unto you. For I have not sent them, saith the* LORD, *yet they prophesy a lie in my name; that I might drive you out, and that ye might perish, ye, and the prophets that prophesy unto you.* Jeremiah 27:14-15. In chapter 28 there was a contest between Hananiah the false prophet and Jeremiah. It was a contest of discernment between true and false prophets. Hananiah, whom had local support, was speaking peace when there was to be no peace. *And Hananiah spake in the presence of all the people, saying, Thus saith the* LORD; *Even so will I break the yoke of Nebuchadnezzar king of Babylon from the neck of all nations within the space of two full years. And the prophet Jeremiah went his way;* Jeremiah 28:11. Jeremiah's message was true and condemning but with a **light of hope** for the future. Jeremiah was speaking the words of God. *Then the word of the* LORD *came unto Jeremiah the prophet, after that Hananiah the prophet had broken the yoke from off the neck of the prophet Jeremiah, saying, Go and tell Hananiah, saying, Thus saith the* LORD; *Thou hast broken the yokes of wood; but thou shalt make for them yokes of iron. For thus saith the* LORD *of hosts, the God of Israel; I have put a yoke of iron upon the neck of all these nations, that they may serve Nebuchadnezzar king of Babylon; and they shall serve him: and I have given him the beasts of the field also;* Jeremiah 28:12-14. Chapter 29 was the letter that Jeremiah wrote and sent to those that were in exile. The Lord instructed the people not to be overcome by the severity of the judgment, but to take heart in a long term promise because He had made up His mind for them to be in 70 years of captivity. They were not to lose their hope but build houses, have children, and live life there for now.

Jeremiah 29: ¹⁰ For thus saith the LORD, *That after seventy years be accomplished at Babylon I will visit you, and perform my good word toward you, in causing you to return to this place. ¹¹ For I know the thoughts that I think toward you, saith the* LORD, *thoughts of peace, and not of evil, to give you an expected end. ¹² Then shall ye call upon me, and ye shall go and pray unto me, and I will hearken unto you. ¹³ And ye shall seek me, and find me, when ye shall search for me with all your heart. ¹⁴ And I will be found of you, saith the* LORD: *and I will turn away your captivity, and I will gather you from all the nations, and from all the places whither I have driven you, saith the* LORD; *and I will bring you again into the place whence I caused you to be carried away captive.* The life that we live here on this earth is our exile until we decide to seek the Lord with all our heart and then we will be brought to a higher place. *But seek ye first the kingdom of God, and his righteousness; and all these things shall be added unto you.* Matthew 6:33. The 70 years of exile is the type of human life span we live, our sojourn time here on this earth. *The days of our years are threescore years and ten; and if by reason of strength they be fourscore years, yet is their strength labour and sorrow; for it is soon cut off, and we fly away.* Psalm 90:10

God cares about every detail in our lives, in fact, *But the very hairs of your head are all numbered;* Matthew 10:30. We sometimes think that God's plan is always going to be a "*feel good"* plan to make us happy. The message that Jeremiah delivered to God's people was very much the opposite of a *"feel good"* plan. God always has a plan that we sometimes do not understand because He works in the impossible. Jeremiah was speaking to a group of people that were being held captive in Babylon. He was letting them know that He has not forgotten them and He has a plan for their lives, even though they are not where they would expect to be or where they would ask God to place them. We have all been in a place or are in a place now that we would not expect to be in or would ask God to place us. When we are in the midst of our own difficult situations, God wants us to know that He has a plan for us all. As we submit to the plan that God has for us He wants to use us to bless those around us; *And ye shall seek me, and find me, when ye shall search for me with all your heart* Jeremiah 29:13. God wants us to know that His plans are not to just benefit us personally. You see, God's plan for Judah was for them to seek the welfare of Babylon because He would not be removing them from their exile anytime soon; *And seek the peace of the city whither I have caused you to be carried away captives, and pray unto the LORD for it: for in the peace thereof shall ye have peace* Jeremiah 29:7. His plan was to restore them back to their own land but it would take 70 years.

When we do things according to God's plan and God's time is right, He will bring you out of your exile. God is the Master Timekeeper, and when He says the time is right then that will be the time for Him to bring us out of our exile. From wherever He has scattered us, He will bring us back and settle us, giving us true rest in His Kingdom.

How does God want you to trust His plan in the midst of life's daily difficulties? How does God want to use you to be a blessing to others?

God wants to give us all an expected end that we pray and hope for, and expect. This kind of end would put an end to all our troubles, and put us in a better place of prosperity to enjoy all good things promised and waited for. When we are not in line with the will of God, we sometimes fear **the plans that God has for us** and think that they are all against us. He knows everything concerning each and every one of us and they are **thoughts of good and not of evil**. To us it may seem evil but when you have God, all things work for your good; *And we know that all things work together for good to them that love God, to them who are the called according to his purpose:* Romans 8:28. All His works and thoughts agree because He does all according to the counsel of His will. Sometimes we don't know our own thoughts or mind but God is never uncertain within Himself. *Known unto God are all his works from the beginning of the world.* Acts 15:18 He promises that He will bring you home and out of exile in due time. His thoughts are working towards the **expected end** and it may not be the end that we expect will come or at the time we want it to come. God asks that we be patient while the fruit ripens before He will give it to us. Our trials and tribulations, troubles or exile may last longer than we want but it does not last always. He wants us to push through even when things seem they are at its worst, they will start to mend and He will see us to the glorious perfection of our deliverance because His work is perfect. *He is the Rock, his work is perfect: for all* *his ways are judgment: a God of truth and without iniquity, just and right is he;* Deuteronomy 32:4

God promises you that you will no longer be in exile. He promises that He will bring you home and give you the promise land. He promises that He will give you His rest. All this will be yours because of the good plans that He has in His heart for you. He wants all this to be given to you, so He requires us to push through our trials and troubles. He wants us to build and strengthen our family ties and also with other families of His people. God wants us to be at peace with all men, so we can grow in righteousness and holiness to produce fruit and transform in His image. As we transform into His image we will have the heart that will seek Him in everything. *And they entered into a covenant to seek the Lord God of their fathers with all their heart and with all their soul;* 2 Chronicles 15:12

No matter what your trials or troubles are today, God has a promise that offers an assurance for your future. It declares His intimate relationship to His people. He will never leave you nor forsake you because He is intricately involved in creating a new future with a perspective of hope. God knows what is best for us. He will lead us in the direction of a new future, because the lies of this world, that sound good, will never get us there. Just as the lies that the false prophet, Hananiah, was speaking to the people of Judah would not prosper them. God wants us to trust Him because He has everything under control. He knows our situations and have our best interest in mind. God knows the future, and His plans are good and full of hope. As long as God, who knows the future, provides our agenda and goes with us as we fulfill His mission, we can have boundless hope. This does not mean that we will be spared pain, suffering, or hardship, but that God will see us through to a glorious future. God's promises are for everyone; He does know the plans He has for us. He loves us and wants us to have a future. He will not harm us.

CHAPTER 8

Eyes Wide Shut

2 Corinthians 5:7 (For we walk by faith, not by sight:)

The Greek word for believe is "Peitho" – it means to persuade, i.e. to induce one by words to believe or persuade by hearing. So then faith cometh by hearing, and hearing by the word of God; Romans 10:17. As we hear the word of God we are persuaded to believe in the Him and the promises that he gives. Abraham is the "Father of Faith" because he was fully persuaded that God would deliver on His promises. You see, our faith always go back to the promises of God because at the root of our faith is God Himself; *He staggered not at the promise of God through unbelief; but was strong in faith, giving glory to God; And being fully persuaded that, what he had promised, he was able also to perform;* Romans 4:20-21

When we *walk by faith* we will see our future prosper the way God sees our future. The trials, troubles and circumstances of this world can distract us from using our faith, the way God uses His faith, to stay focused spiritually in order to see the promises of God. When you believe in God's words, that is how you keep your focus. God will always keep His word. *Let us hold fast the profession of our faith without wavering; (for he is faithful that promised;)* Hebrews 10:23. Our thoughts are no different than His thoughts when we hold fast to confessing God's words in faith. We must look beyond the physical world and take our eyes off the things that is causing our vision to be blurred so we could see what God has spoken for us in the spiritual realm. *Set your affection on things above, not on things on the earth* Colossians 3:2. When we believe on His word He will do what He said He will do. Nothing will ever change the will of God for your life.

Our faith rests on us believing in Him without seeing Him. In this world we are burdened with a body of sin. Our body of flesh is a heavy burden in which our souls dwell. Death will take away our flesh covering, as well as end all our troubles here on earth. We groan because the calamities of life are a heavy burden, but true faith believers shall be clothed with garments of praise and robes of righteousness and glory. God is here with us, by His Spirit, yet we are not with Him as we would like to be. *Therefore we are always confident, knowing that, whilst we are at home in the body, we are absent from the Lord:* 2 Corinthians 5:6. Both the body and the Lord claims a part of us, but the Lord pleads most powerfully to be united with the soul of the believer. This shows clearly;

We are confident, I say, and willing rather to be absent from the body, and to be present with the Lord 2 Corinthians 5:8. What is death, but an object of fear, compared to being absent from the Lord.

As we live, act and conduct ourselves in a certain way in our course of life with reference to the things unseen and not to the things seen, we are doing what the scriptures denote – *To walk. Therefore we are buried with him by baptism into death: that like as Christ was raised up from the dead by the glory of the Father, even so we also should walk in newness of life* Romans 6:4. By faith, we are directed and guided by the Holy Spirit which is invisible, but we believe in its existence. Now that we believe, we walk and live in the confidence of expectation of what is to come according to the word of God. When we don't believe then we walk and live by the flesh which influences us by what we can see. These are the type of people that live by the wealth, honor, splendor, and praise for what they can get from this world. They don't believe or is moved by the unseen. Now on the flip side of this, God is unseen, the Christian or true believer has faith in the reality of the glories of heaven, has faith that there is a Redeemer, has faith that there is a Crown of Glory and will live and act as if they have seen it all. *He that believeth and is baptized shall be saved; but he that believeth not shall be damned* Mark 16:16. With the naked eye, Christ is unseen but we live and act as if we have seen Him in the flesh. We live as if God Himself is watching us daily. The Holy Spirit is unseen but we live and act as if we need it for renewing and purifying of the soul. Heaven is unseen but we live and act as if we know that it exists and have seen its glories. Were these things ever visible to the naked eye as they are to the eye of our faith? No one would doubt the propriety (the state or quality of conforming to conventionally accepted standards of behavior or morals) of living and acting with reference to them. There would be no difference if they really existed and were seen with the naked eye. Whether or not if we see them, it does not change the nature of their importance and just because we do not see them does not change how we live and act toward them.

We have all been influenced by something that was or is unseen, such as, an object we want to purchase in the future, a happiness not yet attained, an honor or wealth not yet accomplished, all which are in the distant future. Furthermore, for the unbeliever even after receiving these things their plans become frustrated and they are utterly disappointed so now their plans fail and offer them nothing that was promised. But this is not so with the believer or Christian, we have the promise of eternal life; once obtained it will not disgust, decay or disappoint, but it will meet all the expectations of the soul. *That if thou shalt confess with thy mouth the Lord Jesus, and shalt believe in thine heart that God hath raised him from the dead, thou shalt be saved* Romans 10:9. The bottom line is that, as Christians, we should not be influenced by the things that we see or governed by our sight. It is by our faith that we are influenced and controlled and not by our sight.

The Apostle Paul said that we live but by our faith when we believe and not by our sight. Faith carries the idea of bring certain and assured of the reality of what is believed. *Now faith is the substance of things hoped for, the evidence of things not seen;* Hebrews 11:1. Through the eye we see nothing but mortality, corruption and misery but through our faith we see a more excellent state of life. Our lives are governed by faith in our immortal hope and not by the outward appearance of worldly things. Faith is the eye of the soul and the hand that receives Christ. It also answers many useful purposes as grace by which it looks to Christ for righteousness, peace, and salvation. Faith is the foot that goes to Christ and walks in Him as it receives Him. Faith is a continued course of believing in the invisible glories of the other world and it is an evidence of things not see.

There is a sense in which sight is involved, it is not that full sight, face to face, but it is the spiritual seeing of faith rather than seeing with the physical eye. Our Christian life is expressive, not of a weak, but of a strong steady faith of glory and happiness and is to be regulated and conducted by our faith. Faith looks at, and has a glimpse of things not seen, which are eternal, as opposed to the external and outward appearances of physical sight which is but seeing as through a glass darkly.

By faith he forsook Egypt, not fearing the wrath of the king: for he endured, as seeing him who is invisible; Hebrews 11:27. Moses had a strong faith in God, which helped him to endure the trials and pains because he could see as if by physical sight the God who is invisible. *No man hath seen God at any time, the only begotten Son, which is in the bosom of the Father, he hath declared him;* John 1:18. Our faith becomes our eyes to see and our ears to hear but mostly it is our guiding force of understanding through the heart. *For this people's heart is waxed gross, and their ears are dull of hearing, and their eyes they have closed; lest at any time they should see with their eyes and hear with their ears, and should understand with their heart, and should be converted, and I should heal them*; Matthew 13:15. Faith allows us to respond to God's promises positively. God's promises must be seen, heard, and understood in the heart so that we may believe and act upon it to bear fruit. Faith, like a mustard see, must be planted, watered, and nurtured.

Hear ye therefore the parable of the sower. When any one heareth the word of the kingdom, and understandeth it not, then cometh the wicked one, and catcheth away that which was sown in his heart. This is he which received seed by the way side. But he that received the seed into stony places, the same is he that heareth the word, and anon with joy receiveth it; Yet hath he not root in himself, but dureth for a while: for when tribulation or persecution ariseth because of the word, by and by he is offended. He also that received seed among the thorns is he that heareth the word; and the care of this world, and the deceitfulness of riches, choke the word, and he becometh unfruitful. But he that received seed into the good ground is he that heareth the word, and understandeth it; which also beareth fruit, and bringeth forth, some an hundredfold, some sixty, some thirty; Matthew 13:18-23.

If we continue to "walk by sight", our experiences are what we depend upon for authority instead of depending on the visions we see and the voice we hear. *For the Son of Man is as a man taking a far journey, who left his house, and gave authority to his servants, and to every man his work, and commanded the porter to watch;* Mark 13:34. Most of us are more dominated by our sight than we are by our faith. Our continued dependency upon our senses for authority is dangerous. For those that choose to "walk by sight", God allows delusions not of divine origin upon those who "do not believe the truth"; *Even him, whose coming is after the working of Satan with all power and signs and lying wonders, And with all deceivableness of unrighteousness in them that perish; because they received not the love of the truth, that they might be saved. And for this cause God shall send them strong delusion, that they should believe a lie: That they all might be damned who believed not the truth, but had pleasure in unrighteousness;* 2 Thessalonians 2:9-12. Too many of us place our minds on accumulating certain wealth over serving God. This is understandable when you walk by sight and all you can see is what money and its accompanied pleasures it bring, but you cannot see God. Man's eyes are never satisfied; *Hell and destruction are never full; so the eyes of man are never satisfied;* Proverbs 27:20 and now this wealth becomes a god; *No man can serve two masters: for either he will hate the one, and love the other; or else he will hold to the one, and despise the other. Ye cannot serve God and mammon;* Matthew 6:24. Paul told Timothy to instruct the rich not to have strong moral principles on the uncertainty of riches, which brings man into ruin and destruction, but in the living God; *Charge them that are rich in this world, that they be not highminded, nor trust in uncertain riches, but in the living God, who giveth us richly all things to enjoy;* 1 Timothy 6:17.

When we "walk by faith", we trust in revelation for authority. When we renew ourselves to the point that faith dominates sight, then miracles happen. When we let the word of God or scriptures direct us then we are truly "walking by faith". Peter emphasized his authority as an eyewitness not only because of what he saw on the Mount of Transfiguration but also because of the prophetic word of God. The Bible is God's very word given to man to give to all people. The righteous that walk by faith handles this world's goods with contentment because it is God that gives us power to get wealth; *But thou shalt remember the LORD thy God: for it is he that giveth thee power to get wealth, that he may establish his covenant which he sware unto thy fathers, as it is this day;* Deuteronomy 8:18. These are the people that place God at the forefront of their lives because they know that God has promised to supply our needs through our faith; *But my God shall supply all your need according to his riches in glory by Christ Jesus;* Philippians 4:19

Asaph was said to be David's music director and his demands for justice and equality almost caused his steps to slip when he saw the wicked prosper; *But as for me, my feet were almost gone; my steps had well nigh slipped. For I was envious at the foolish, when I saw the prosperity of the wicked.* Psalm 73:2-3. Just as some of us do now that wonder why the wicked prosper and the righteous live according to the word of God still suffer so much. This is not what the righteous children of God should be worrying about because our faith will falter like Asaph's. Our "walk by faith" will help us face the sufferings of today. Now we know that Paul was no foolish visionary. Paul was one that faced his sufferings head on and still his deepest concern was the church; *Of the Jews five times received I forty stripes save one. Thrice was I beaten with rods, once was I stoned, thrice I suffered shipwreck, a night and a day I have been in the deep; In journeyings often, in perils of waters, in perils of robbers, in perils by mine own countrymen, in perils by the heathen, in perils in the city, in perils in the wilderness, in perils in the sea, in perils among false brethren; In weariness and painfulness, in watchings often, in hunger and thirst, in fastings often, in cold and nakedness. Beside those things that are without, that which cometh upon me daily, the care of all the churches* 2 Corinthians 11:24-28. Paul di not despair during his time of sufferings because his eye of faith was set on heaven and not on this world; *For which cause we faint not; but though our outward man perish, yet the inward man is renewed day by day. For our light affliction, which is but for a moment, worketh for us a far more exceeding and eternal weight of glory; While we look not at the things which are seen, but at the things which are not seen: for the things which are seen are temporal; but the things which are not seen are eternal* 2 Corinthians 4:16-18.

The Bible challenges us to "walk by faith, not by sight." This is as unnatural as walking with our eyes closed. But the more steps we take, the more comfortable this walk will be come, and the more confident we will be of the destination of our walk. And ultimately that's what faith is all about – it is "the assurance of things hoped for."

CHAPTER 9

More Than a Bosom Can Hold

Luke 6: [38] Give, and it shall be given unto you; good measure, pressed down, and shaken together, and running over, shall men give into your bosom. For with the same measure that ye mete withal it shall be measured to you again.

A good measure is what's known as a full measure. Press down, just as you do to place more in a container, you press it down to get more in it. When you shake something to make all the contents become compact to get more into it. Running over where you receive more than you expect. God will then cause men to give into your bosom as a reward for you giving to those that are in need. When you are kind and giving to God's people then God's people are kind and giving to you. When they give they will give into your bosom. A Bosom is a large pocket on the front of long, wide and loose garments that were worn by Oriental nations so that things could be carried in them, which their hands could not contain, hence the purpose of pockets. *And the LORD said furthermore unto him, Put now thine hand into thy bosom. And he put his hand into his bosom: and when he took it out, behold, his hand was leprous as snow. And he said, Put thine hand into thy bosom again. And he put his hand into his bosom again; and plucked it out of his bosom, and, behold, it was turned again as his other flesh;* Exodus 4:6-7. With garments of this kind, they could receive into their bosom a considerable amount of dry goods such as wheat or corn til it overflows. In the Eastern markets you could see vendors pouring the contents of a dry measure into the bosom of a purchaser. *Also he said, Bring the vail that thou hast upon thee, and hold it. And when she held it, he measured six measures of barley, and laid it on her: and she went into the city;* Ruth 3:15. The gathered fold of the wide upper garment, bound together with the girdle, and thus forming a pouch.

Because we honor God's words, He gives a special blessing where He will cause men to give into your bosom just the same as you give into others. When you are steadfast and unmovable in God's word, He don't just bless you with any measure but He blesses you with good measure. God is always faithful to His promises. He will take care of those that are obedient to His will by rewarding them plentifully and fully; *Blessed is he that considereth the poor: the LORD will deliver him in time of trouble. The LORD will preserve him, and keep him alive; and he shall be blessed upon the earth: and thou wilt not deliver him unto the will of his enemies. The LORD will strengthen him upon the bed of languishing: thou wilt make all his bed in his sickness.* Psalm 41:1-3. God Himself will reward those that do charitable and merciful acts by blessing them with His unexpected providential (involving divine foresight or intervention) dispensation (an act of providing something to people). *When thou cuttest down thine harvest in thy field, and hast forgot a sheaf in the field, thou shalt not go again to fetch it: it shall be for the stranger, for the fatherless, and for the widow: that the* LORD *thy God may bless thee in all the work of thine hands;* Deuteronomy 24:19. *But this I say, He which soweth sparingly shall reap also sparingly; and he which soweth bountifully shall reap also bountifully;* 2 Corinthians 9:6. When God causes men to give unto you, it is good measure, pressed down, shaken together and running over. There is no good measure than to keep shaking of the bushel to get more from it, the pressing down of dry corn to get more into your bosom, and the pouring of the wheat til the measure runneth over. If we learn to give freely of our worldly goods to those that are in need according to our ability then it shall be returned with great recompense. *The Lord recompense thy work, and a full reward be given thee of the Lord God of Israel, under whose wings thou art come to trust;* Ruth 2:12.

Among the Jews, they reference to dry measure because liquid will not agree to the terms of good measure, pressed down, and shaken together. With their methods of measuring, they thrust and press to make it hold more, shake it also for the same purpose, and then they would heap it up as much as they could til it fall over. Some of their measures they heaped (to put (something) in a large pile) in a pile or mound, and some they did not. All the measures in the Sanctuary, were heaped, except the high Priest's. There were two decimaries (tithing vessels) in the sanctuary, one was "heaped" and the other was "stricken". With respect to this distinction of measures, they do not strike in the place where they heap, nor heap in the place where they strike. When the Jews measured corn, wheat and barley they did it in a rather forceful way, by slamming it down, shaking it together to get the chaffs out, press it down and then heap it into a pile. *Whose fan is in his hand, and he will throughly purge his floor, and gather his wheat into the garner; but he will burn up the chaff with unquenchable fire;* Matthew 3:12.

It is more blessed to give than to receive; *I have shewed you all things, how that so labouring ye ought to support the weak, and to remember the words of the Lord Jesus, how he said, It is more blessed to give than to receive* Acts 20:35. Every Christian should have a heart for giving. When we see people that are in need of alms or aid, we should minister unto the requests with overflowing generosity and not grudgingly. We should never short change the poor by skimping on the measure of alms given nor do the same in your giving to the church. Short changing and making the ephah small was condemned by God's prophets; *Saying, When will the new moon be gone, that we may sell corn? and the sabbath, that we may set forth wheat, making the **ephah small**, and the shekel great, and falsifying the balances by deceit?* Amos 8:5. Anything done in faith and obedience to God will produce an increase. Can we be content with less than the very largest measure or best. We must give then to man, what we desire to receive of God. God knows how much each and every one of us have to give so it is with great disrespect to God to do little when you could do more. This is why we reap what we sow; *Be not deceived; God is not mocked: for whatsoever a man soweth, that shall he also reap. For he that soweth to his flesh shall of the flesh reap corruption; but he that soweth to the Spirit shall of the Spirit reap life everlasting. And let us not be weary in well doing: for in due season we shall reap, if we faint not;* Galatians 6:7-9.

Most people think that when you give, it has to be money but it can be money, our possessions, love, a prayer and even our time. Just as we plant seed into the ground to receive back more seeds or harvest, so it is with everything we give. We reap what we sow and receive the same amount (measure) that we give; *But this I say, He which soweth sparingly shall reap also sparingly; and he which soweth bountifully shall reap also bountifully;* 2 Corinthians 9:6. Whatever we sow it shall return back unto us whether it be positive or negative; *Judge not, and ye shall not be judged: condemn not, and ye shall not be condemned: forgive, and ye shall be forgiven:* Luke 6:7. The negative that we sow does not have to come back unto us if we apply the greater law of forgiveness; *If we confess our sins, he is faithful and just to forgive us our sins, and to cleanse us from all unrighteousness.* 1 John 1:9. Our positive that we sow we can miss out on it returning back to us if we don't continue in well doing; *And let us not be weary in well doing: for in due season we shall reap, if we faint not.* Galatians 6:9. If we are late in our giving then our return will be late. We must move when God tells us to move and not when we think we should give or else our seed will be sowed in bad soil. If we give grudgingly, it will be given to us grudgingly. If we give cheerfully then it will be given to us cheerfully; *Every man according as he purposeth in his heart, so let him give; not grudgingly, or of necessity: for God loveth a cheerful giver.* 2 Corinthians 9:7. Although God is our source for everything, He would use people for His will. We must believe that the Lord hears and answers our prayers so that He would send His people to sow into our bosoms.

Our giving should be for the sake of God and not for our own interest or out of mere human generosity because it is He who engages Himself to pay these debts of His people with true unlimited generosity. When God commands us to give to our neighbors, He does so by the prospect of a reward. We live in a time where mutual help is necessary but our self-interest, pride and other corrupt evil doings cause us to offend each other. We must humble ourselves so that the help needed from our neighbors will come without strife. If we don't humble ourselves and give up some things, then we will render life itself unsupportable. Without a giving or forging spirit then there will be nothing but divisions, evil surmising, anger, vengeance and total dissolution among the body of Christ. Our interest in both the Spiritual and Physical world calls for us to give and forgive. God is so serious about our generosity and giving to others that He warns us that our measure of treating and judging others will be the basis used for measuring and treating us by others and by God. God is so gracious to us and our blessings are based on our willingness to bless others. Now, we can either share that graciousness or abuse it.

Let's get to the jist of what Luke 6:38 means: If you read verses 27-37, Christ was referring to loving our enemies, giving to those in need, and for those that smite thee, we must turn and offer the other cheek. He was also saying that we must forgive those that hate, curse and use us. Christ is teaching us that we will receive back if we give generously. It does not say when we will receive the blessing or how much. In verse 38 it says **"it shall be given unto you"**, which is future tense. This could be tomorrow, next week, next month, next year or even years from now. Only God knows when you will receive. **"Shall men give"** is a third person, plural and future tense which really means, "they will give". God will give unmerited earthly blessings according to the phrase **"into your bosom"**. Bosom means "kolpos" in Greek which is the area for carrying or holding material goods. Too many of us, Christians, think that God will always give the same exact measure that they give money or material things to others. We need to stop thinking that God does not give to those that do not give to the needy or to churches because according to Luke 6:35 *But love ye your enemies, and do good, and lend, hoping for nothing again; and your reward shall be great, and ye shall be the children of the Highest: for he is kind unto the unthankful and to the evil,* and Matthew 5:45 *That ye may be the children of your Father which is in heaven: for he maketh his sun to rise on the evil and on the good, and sendeth rain on the just and on the unjust,* God gives good gifts to evil, unrighteous and unthankful people.

In Luke 6:27-37 Christ was teaching us to avoid such things as bondage, carnality, and selfishness that we fall into by miss using the God given unmerited grace that He gives us in Luke 6:38. Forgiveness of sin is by God's undeserved grace and mercy. The measure of you forgiving and forgiveness will be given back to you is partly related to *"For with the same measure that ye mete withal it shall be measured to you again"* in Luke 6:38. Our deservance of God's forgiveness because we forgive others is the condition on which He will forgive us by His underserved grace. Because this condition is God determined, fulfilling it will result in a promised manifestation of God's unmerited grace. God is kind and merciful to evil people. He asks us to be the same in Luke 6:27-36. God will show His unmerited grace and mercy to those that show love, grace and mercy to others.

In the Greek language "misthos" means "pay, wages, reward" or "a recompense based upon what a person has earned and thus deserves". Christ used the word reward in Luke 6:35 where He was referring to God rewarding believers based on how they treat those that hate, curse, hit and use them. These rewards are those given by God the Father as part of His training and discipline of His children but are not the deserved rewards that someone who perfectly obeyed God every moment of every day would be owed by God's perfect justice.

CHAPTER 10

Giving Thanks is a Must

1 Thessalonians 5:18 In every thing give thanks: for this is the will of God in Christ Jesus concerning you.

This was written by Paul to the church in Thessalonica that he himself established. He wrote the letter or epistle to the Thessalonians to express his thanks for all that God had done in them, and to encourage them to not give up on their faith even when times get hard and uneasy. It says that we are to give thanks unto God the Father, in the name of Jesus Christ in all things. It did not say for some things or most things but it said for all things. Even during our trials and adversities we should give thanks just as Job did. When we are in positions or circumstances that are uncomfortable or unagreeable with us, we need to give thanks unto God almighty because it could be worse and it could be that God is trying to get you to see something about yourself. When we are under the temptations of Satan, which could be great and heavy, we should give praise because the Lord said unto us, *my **grace is sufficient** for thee: for my strength is made perfect in weakness. Most gladly therefore will I rather glory in my infirmities, that the power of Christ may rest upon me,* 2 Corinthians 12:9 and it is sufficient to bear under them and will deliver you out of them all.

This means the good as well as the bad. This means in all and every affliction, since we know that God works all things together for the good of those that love the Lord. Since He is in total control and He allows both good and bad things to come to us, we must give praise **in every situation**. Whenever God is working it then you can best believe that there is always a blessing to come in the end. He wants us to stay in prayer because when we *Confess our faults one to another, and pray one for another, that ye may be healed. The effectual fervent prayer of a righteous man availeth much* James 5:16.

If we look at the difference between giving God thanks "for" everything and "in" everything, we will see that we are not to give thanks "for" everything because that would mean that we give thanks for Satan and all the corruption that he causes. When we look at Job's situation in chapter 1 verse 21, he worshipped God and not cursed Him, *And said, Naked came I out of my mother's womb, and naked shall I return thither: the LORD gave, and the LORD hath taken away; blessed be the name of the LORD.* Although all that was happening was being rendered by Satan but God allowed it to test the faith of Job and then verse 22 shows that Satan was wrong and sorely defeated because Job praised God "in" his situation. *In all this Job sinned not, nor charged God foolishly.* Job 1:22

Now don't think that because something bad is happening in your life it is always God's will. When Paul wrote this scripture he was not saying that everything that happens in your life is God's will. What Paul was trying to get us to understand was that we are to praise God "in" every situation, trial or circumstance, but not "for" every situation, trial or circumstance. Paul never meant or never anticipated that we would believe that rape, murder, abuse and fornication are all things sent from God for which we are to give thanks unto Our Father for. Paul is teaching that all bad things in our lives is not the will of God but was encouraging thanksgiving unto God. We are to give thanks always in all things. When you doctor visit turns into one that you are told that you have cancer, it is very difficult to give thanks for that. What we need to do is have an attitude like Samuel had when he said, *And Samuel told him every whit, and hid nothing from him. And he said, It is the LORD: let him do what seemeth him good* 1 Samuel 3:18. We are to give thanks in our situations.

Our giving of thanks and giving praise are very closely related because it is literally impossible to give thanks unto the Lord without praising Him for what He has done, what He is doing and what He will do. All things work according to the will of God, otherwise He would prevent it. God measures out the right amount of faith (*For I say, through the grace given unto me, to every man that is among you, not to think of himself more highly than he ought to think; but to think soberly, according as*

God hath dealt to every man the measure of faith. Romans 12:3) to every person just like He knows how to give just the right amount of sunshine and rain when needed. His divine power mixes the bitter and sweet, the good and evil, in just the right amount so that they would work together for our good. He measures out those with great precision.

Because of His goodness, we have a reason to make our humble complaints to God, we never can have any reason to complain of God. We always have much reason to praise and give thanks. As we must in everything *be careful for nothing; but in everything by prayer and supplication with thanksgiving let your requests be made known unto God.* Philippians 4:16 This is pleasing to God. We should know that thanksgiving should not be just a matter of celebrating a special day once a year but it is to be the ongoing, everyday praise unto the Lord. This verse is a command from God that our thanks be rendered unto Him.

"Father, I don't like what's happening to me and it feels like everything is falling apart. To be honest, I wish that none of this had ever happened to me. I'm afraid but I know that you are in total control, so why would you let something like this happen to me. I know your faithfulness in never ending and that you are the same yesterday, today and forever more. I know that nothing is too hard for you and my end result will be nothing but good. So Father I give you all praise, honor and glory because of your truths. I thank you in this situation in the name of your matchless and perfect Son, Jesus Christ, Amen.

CHAPTER 11

We Must Make a Decision

Joshua 24: [15] And if it seem evil unto you to serve the LORD, choose you this day whom ye will serve; whether the gods which your fathers served that were on the other side of the flood, or the gods of the Amorites, in whose land ye dwell: but as for me and my house, we will serve the LORD.

What is known in the Bible about Joshua's family? Nothing. No matter what we know about His family, Joshua has commanded that him and his family will serve the Lord. No descendant or member of his household is named in the Bible.1 Chronicles 7:20-29 lists the descendants of Ephraim but Joshua is the last in his own line. Joshua was part of a house that included all the faithful servants of the Lord. *But Christ as a son over his own house; whose house are we, if we hold fast the confidence and the rejoicing of the hope firm unto the end.* Hebrews 3:6

We need to ask ourselves, "What would seem evil about serving the almighty true living God? Joshua was implying that worshipping God was necessary and reasonable and to put away all idolatry in themselves. We worship idols and not even know it. When we do things that take us out of being in the presence of the Lord it becomes an idol, for example: television binge watching, secular music, your job, etc...... His words may sound like a powerful insinuation. But you see, God gives them the freedom to make their own decisions but they were bound by the Law of Moses to give their worship t God only. We now are not bound by the Law of Moses because Christ came as man, was hung on the cross and died but rose three days later so that we could be bound by the Salvation that was freely given to us but cost Jesus Christ an unrepayable price. Joshua was trying to get them to understand that worshipping God is beneficial and every man in his right mind should choose to serve God before any idol. So that our worship to God will be in spirit and truth we must be free and willing to serve God and not be forced or pushed. Our love for God will make our service to Him acceptable in His sight. *Now the God of peace, that brought again from the dead our Lord Jesus, that great shepherd of the sheep, through the blood of the everlasting covenant, Make you perfect in every good work to do his will, working in you that which is wellpleasing in his sight, through Jesus Christ; to whom be glory for ever and ever. Amen.* Hebrews 13:20-21

We put enmity against God when our minds are carnal (not spiritual; merely human; temporal; worldly) and therefore our spiritual worship is null and void. Just the same as God put enmity between the serpent and the woman (*And I will put enmity between thee and the woman, and between thy seed and her seed; it shall bruise thy head, and thou shalt bruise his heel.* Genesis 3:15). For the sin that was committed then and for the sins we commit now, God sent His only begotten Son to die for us to be born again.

Joshua laid before the people a choice that they must make "Choose you this day whom you will serve", the choice is still laid before each and every one of us today whether you understand or not who God is. When we reach that point of understanding what it means to serve God then we must do it in sincerity and truth. Now, this can only be done from a free and willing heart. Before Joshua gave the choice Moses had done so as well. Joshua had called on the people of Israel in a public and solemn manner to declare that they will be faithful and obedient unto God. He asked them to make an open statement of affirmation," to put away the strange gods that were among them". We too must make an open and solemn statement of affirmation when we confess "*with thy mouth the Lord Jesus, and shalt believe in thine heart that God hath raised him from the dead, thou shalt be saved.* Romans 10:9. Elijah had also challenged the people on Carmel "*And Elijah came unto all the people, and said, How long halt ye between two opinions? If the* LORD *be God, follow him: but if Baal, then follow him. And the people answered him not a word* 1 Kings 18:21.

What shall I render unto the Lord for all his **benefits** toward me? Psalm 116:12 Now that you have chosen to serve the

Lord you should seek Him by reading His word to find out who He is and then all the benefits will be given unto you. *But seek ye first the kingdom of God, and his righteousness; and all these things shall be added unto you.* Matthew 6:33 We are faced with enormous decisions each and every day but let me reassure you that, to choose God almighty will be the best decision you will make. Joshua told the people that as for him and his house, they will serve the Lord. Now if you feel that you can truly find a better God that is more pleasant and profitable then you choose you this day whom you will serve. Remember now that the true almighty living God is a jealous God.

Sometimes we must take the lead, no matter what people say or no matter their decision, and move forward in our spiritual roles to guide and direct the lost to Christ. What Joshua was doing was preparing the people of Israel for the land of Canaan (Promise land). Joshua would stand firm in his faith in God against the greatest odds to serve God although he was concerned about the people of Israel. It was very clear that Joshua's first priority was his family then the people of Israel. Joshua's lead is an example for all men to learn from and follow. Joshua was setting an example for the people of Israel to follow when he said, "but as for me and my house, we will serve the Lord". Abraham had also commanded his household that they shall keep the way of the Lord as well. *For I know him, that he will command his children and his household after him, and they shall keep the way of the LORD, to do justice and judgment; that the LORD may bring upon Abraham that which he hath spoken of him.* Genesis 18:19

We need to make a decision and stop putting it off til tomorrow or when you feel that you are ready. If you wait til then, then you will never be ready. God is a faithful and true God that will never leave you nor forsake you so if you decide to walk in the way of the Lord you will wish you had done it years ago. *Let your conversation be without covetousness; and be content with such things as ye have: for he hath said, I will never leave thee, nor forsake thee* Hebrews 13:5. So what are you waiting for? If you are ready to serve the Lord and do His will then say this prayer:

Heavenly Father, I come to do your will and not mine because you are God of grace and Lord of Mercy, I will follow your lead and your direction. I choose you to be Lord over my life because no matter where I search I cannot find another God like you. For you are God and God alone and there is no other God. As I walk the path that you have make for me I ask that you be a light unto my path and a lamp unto my feet. I refuse to stumble as I walk in your ways. You are my stronghold and my Hightower and my shelter in the storm. I give you all the honor, all the praise and all the glory and this I pray in the matchless name of your Son, Jesus Christ, Amen.

CHAPTER 12

The Hidden Blessings

Hebrews 11:1-3 Now faith is the substance of things hoped for, the evidence of things not seen. For by it the elders obtained a good report. Through faith we understand that the worlds were framed by the word of God, so that things which are seen were not made of things which do appear.

So many of us have asked the question "What is Faith?" Well, faith is confidence or trust in a person or thing: or the observance of an obligation from loyalty; or a belief not based on proof.

Hope is to cherish a desire with anticipation; hope implies little certainty but suggests confidence or assurance in the possibility that what one desires or longs for will happen. Hope is an optimistic attitude of mind based on an expectation of positive outcome related to events and circumstances in one's life or the world at large.

As you can see, faith and hope go hand in hand. Hope is the confidence and assurance that God will do exactly what He said He would do and keep every promise He has given. *God is not a man, that he should lie; neither the son of man, that he should repent: hath he said, and shall he not do it? or hath he spoken, and shall he not make it good?* Numbers 23:19. Now, our hope is imperfect because we put limits on stuff while our God has no limits, so we fail to do what we said we would do. *Not boasting of things without our measure, that is, of other men's labours; but having hope, when your faith is increased, that we shall be enlarged by you according to our rule abundantly,* 2 Corinthians 10:15. There is hope beyond human hope and this is called Supernatural hope because it directs you to the Almighty God who is true to His word and all powerful (Omnipotent). Jesus is God's visible proof that His word is true, His love is unfailing and unconditional, and His power is immeasurable and unlimited. Our faith is always put to the test every day and it is our hope that helps us to persevere through all trials, difficulties and afflictions. As we persevere through all these things without wavering, *And not only so, but we glory in tribulations also: knowing that tribulation worketh patience; And patience, experience; and experience, hope: And hope maketh not ashamed; because the love of God is shed abroad in our hearts by the Holy Ghost which is given unto us* Romans 5:3-5, then God will give us the gift of Hope to strengthen our faith.

God will reveal Himself to us through the reading of His word to give us the assurance and conviction that His power, presence and glory is more real than what our natural physical eyes can see. We are saved by grace through faith. Faith saves us, doctrine dictates how faith must be applied and if it is not applied correctly then it has no affect. All faith must be in the exact words of God, or else it has no power. The power of our faith is the word of God. The word of God is truth and it is very important when it comes to our faith. *So then **faith** cometh **by hearing**, and **hearing by** the word of God* Romans 10:17.

If we look at the context of the verse, "Now, faith is the substance of the things hoped for, the evidence of things not seen", we see that our faith is holding on to the word of God so that it will give substance to what is not seen in the promises that God gives. Also through our faith we are being guided by the word of God and those things that are unseen are brought to the proof or received with full conviction so we *calleth those things which be not as though they were* Romans 4:17. If we genuinely use our faith, then it would be an act of the whole man and not just our affection, our own will or our own understanding, but all three. Our faith is the instrument that the Spirit has its way through us and thereby we are able to overcome any sin, trial or circumstance. *But Jesus beheld them, and said unto them, With men this is impossible; but with God all things are possible* Matthew 19:26.

When we say that "faith is the substance of things hoped for", we are saying that faith is the principle exercise of our mind and soul that the things that are not seen but hoped for are represented as being without substance. The things that we hope for do not yet exist, since they still belong to the future, *For we are saved by hope: but hope that is seen is not hope: for what a man seeth, why doth he yet hope for?*

25 But if we hope for that we see not, then do we with patience wait for it Romans 8:24-25, are not just figments of our imagination because their basis is the word of God.

Our faith is what proves to our minds that the reality of the things that we cannot see with the natural eye is approved by God to be holy, just and good. Since the beginning of time our faith has caused the truth of God to be received by many examples of persons that have obtained a good report, just as with Noah, Abraham, Joseph, Joshua, etc….. Faith was the principle of their holy obedience and patient sufferings. Now! Right Now! When we speak of NOW we are speaking of right now and not yesterday or tomorrow. We are to use our faith now, now that we understand how to exercise our faith now we must stay encouraged and persevere in doing so.

What is the substance of things hoped for? Confidence - full trust; belief in the powers, trustworthiness, or reliability of a person or thing. So it is our confidence that we will receive all the things that we hope for, *For we are made partakers of Christ, if we hold the beginning of our confidence stedfast unto the end;* Hebrews 3:14. As we persevere in our faith to expect the things we hope for, we are justified and adopted into God's family, born of God's spirit and therefore being His children we are heirs of the things that we hope for. Some of the things that we hope for are; happiness with Jesus Christ after death; our glorious resurrection at the time of Jesus Christ's second coming; and to spread glory with Him in the new heavens and new earth forever.

Now faith is the substance of things hoped for is the general nature of all true faith as stated in Mark 16:16 *He that believeth and is baptized shall be saved; but he that believeth not shall be damned.* We must remember that only faith and not baptism is essential for salvation, as the omission of baptism from the last part of the scripture shows. You see, our eternal life depends on the existence and exercising of our faith.

When you think of things not seen you think of something invisible or something you will never see but what we are talking about are the eternal things of God. Our evidence is a demonstration or proof that truly convinces our understanding and determines our will to follow the word of God. *Trust in the Lord with all thine heart; and **lean not** unto thine own understanding. In all thy ways acknowledge him, and he shall direct thy paths* Proverbs 3:5-6. No matter what it may look like, with our faith being hindered on the power of God, the evidence is the things that God has declared happened or will happen. Our faith is much more than our hope because our hope is things future and attached to good as where our faith is future, present and past and those things that are good or evil. Our faith is the chief principle of living unto God and obtaining the promises and inheriting eternal life.

The word "evidence" means something which shows that something else exists or is true; a visible sign of something; something that furnishes proof. Now do our faith accept or reject what is being said about those things that are unseen. If our faith deals with it as things seen, then we accept that which has stood the proof. The evidence is the conviction in our minds to know that God will never leave us nor forsake us and He will keep every promise He has given.

A true Christian believes what the word of God says. Although we have never seen the Almighty, have never seen an angel or heaven and we have never seen a body raised from the dead. But we have, from the reading of God's word, true evidence in our minds that God has spoken on these things. Because we believe and stand on the words that God has spoken through His word there is no more convincing proof needed that He is the Almighty Creator. Our minds convince us to act as if these declarations of God are so because of the faith that we now build by reading His word. Our unwavering confidence in God sustains our souls that now leads us to act upon the hidden blessings and promises of the things that are unseen.

CHAPTER 13

Who is Leading You?

Romans 8:14 For as many as are led by the Spirit of God, they are the sons of God.

Sonship and heirship, no a joint heirship in the glory of Christ is what we received from the Holy Spirit when we admitted, no, when we created a special relationship with God. Our Christian transformation from the old to the new sonship can be seen in Galatians 4:1-7. *Now I say, That the heir, as long as he is a child, differeth nothing from a servant, though he be lord of all; But is under tutors and governors until the time appointed of the father. Even so we, when we were children, were in bondage under the elements of the world: But when the fulness of the time was come, God sent forth his Son, made of a woman, made under the law, To redeem them that were under the law, that we might receive the adoption of sons. And because ye are sons, God hath sent forth the Spirit of his Son into your hearts, crying, Abba, Father. Wherefore thou art no more a servant, but a son; and if a son, then an heir of God through Christ.*

We all have an ownership in Christ's glory, that is those in which the sonship has been awakened and kept alive by the Holy Spirit. At first we were servants to a schoolmaster but now we are children to the most high God partaking of His nature being spiritually begotten of Him. *But before faith came, we were kept under the law, shut up unto the faith which should afterwards be revealed. Wherefore the law was our schoolmaster to bring us unto Christ, that we might be justified by faith. But after that faith is come, we are no longer under a schoolmaster.* Galatians 3:23-25

It says that "For as many as are led by the Spirit of God, they are the sons of God." For as many means, whosoever is led by the Spirit receives the benefits of the gospel which is the Spirit of adoption. The Apostle speaks of the Spirit as being gracious, loving, leading and a power that helps believers mortify sin. Now that sin is mortified, we shall live as sons of God. The Apostle does not say, as many that live by the Spirit but, for as many as are led by the Spirit, this is saying that the Spirit must be the guide and ruler in our lives. Just as a car has no direction if it has no driver, so are we lost because we have no direction. Once the driver occupies the seat and takes control of the steering then the car has direction and purpose, so as we are when we are led by the Spirit because we cannot see our way unless the Holy Spirit directs us. We have not the strength nor the direction to do God's will unless the Holy Spirit assists us but it will not push us against our own will. *Trust in the Lord with all thine heart; and **lean not unto thine own understanding***. Proverbs 3:5

Before our conversions we were not willing and were led by the Spirit of this world or the devil through darkness but now made willing by the Holy Spirit. The Holy Spirit now leads us from sin, depending on His righteousness, into paths of faith and truth that we did not know of while being led by Satan, but once converted we are so willing that we desire and pray to be led by the Spirit. *Lead me in thy truth, and teach me: for thou art the God of my salvation; on thee do I wait all the day.* Psalm 25:5

We are led to the person, blood, and righteousness of Christ to accept our full salvation and the fullness of His grace. Now that the Holy Spirit bear witness with our Spirit, we are joint heirs with Christ so that we may suffer and be glorified with Him to our final inheritance with Him. *And be found in him, not having mine own righteousness, which is of the law, but that which is through the faith of Christ, the righteousness which is of God by faith: That I may know him, and the power of his resurrection, and the fellowship of his sufferings, being made conformable unto his death;* Philippians 3:9-10

We are Christians who believe on Christ and are led by the Holy Spirit that now receive the spirit of adoption which is an assurance of our conversions with a sonship relation to God. Now we have a confidence to approach the Father as servile - very obedient and trying too hard to please someone, of or suitable to a slave and dutiful children being led by the Holy

Spirit. It is now our duty to walk after the Spirit and not the flesh because the righteousness of Christ has been imparted unto us to secure our soul from death.

What the Spirit does is influence us from above and draws us away from corrupting passions and vanities of this world. We are now sons of God to desire and yield to the influence of the Spirit and be directed in the path of purity and life. Because God will not lead us astray, our yielding to the influence of the Spirit brings our peace and happiness and we are willing to be driven by this unseen hand to obey and cheerfully mortify our pride, destroy lust, humble ambition, and destroy the love of this world.

CHAPTER 14

Seek Out Your Blessings

Matthew 6:33 But seek ye first the kingdom of God, and his righteousness; and all these things shall be added unto you.

What does it mean to seek ye first the Kingdom of God? It means that we are to seek the higher spiritual life in its completeness. The primary subject of the Sermon on the Mount is the Kingdom of God. The Kingdom that our Lord is erecting in this fallen world and should be diligently sought after. We seek His righteousness through prayer and it will be His gift to us. When we seek the Kingdom of God and His righteousness and not our own righteousness then we are submitting ourselves to Him. *For they being ignorant of God's righteousness, and going about to establish their own righteousness, have not submitted themselves unto the righteousness of God.* Romans 10:3

As we are directed through this life by the Spirit, we place all things in His hands and all things that pertain to this life shall be given unto us. *Casting all your care upon him; for he careth for you.* 1 Peter 5:7 Now that we are new Christians we have more to think about, than what we are to wear or eat or drink, because we now have a knowledge of the Father who knows that He will provide all our needs and we need not be anxious for anything. *Be careful for nothing; but in every thing by prayer and supplication with thanksgiving let your requests be made known unto God.* Philippians 4:6 Our focus should be on the Father so that if we put Him and His Kingdom first all these things will be added unto us without us asking. Just because we go to church on Sunday and/or Wednesday or even do good to love our neighbors, which are things of putting God first we can still be tempted to put things before God.

We are constantly tempted so therefore we are on a constant battle between what God expects of us and what we think we need. It's not an easy task of putting God first because things like our jobs, hobbies, family and friends, issues of immorality, etc.., can easily take first place. While we struggle with temptations and various weaknesses in our lives, there is another temptation that we often fail at, and that is the temptation of not trusting God when things seem to not go right or not go our way. We must take no thought for our own life but give it to God because our time is in His hands and no one knows us like He does. *And fear not them which kill the body, but are not able to kill the soul: but rather fear him which is able to destroy both soul and body in hell. Are not two sparrows sold for a farthing? and one of them shall not fall on the ground without your Father. But the very hairs of your head are all numbered. Fear ye not therefore, ye are of more value than many sparrows.* Matthew 10:28-31 We need not worry about tomorrow as it may never come. God has given us life and given us our body so shall He take them back. *And the LORD God formed man of the dust of the ground, and breathed into his nostrils the breath of life; and man became a living soul.* Genesis 2:7

Our God is a jealous God and demands our full attention, even if it means that we are criticized, beaten or even cast out by others, even if it means to speak up for the Holy name of Jesus Christ even if everyone else is silent, even if we are pressured by our peers to not believe on the name of Jesus Christ. *These things I command you, that ye love one another. If the world hate you, ye know that it hated me before it hated you. If ye were of the world, the world would love his own: but because ye are not of the world, but I have chosen you out of the world, therefore the world hateth you. Remember the word that I said unto you, The servant is not greater than his lord. If they have persecuted me, they will also persecute you; if they have kept my saying, they will keep yours also.* John 15:17-20 We have a duty to defend His name in word and in action.

When we seek the Lord our God, He will arm us against the temptations of this world and allow none to move us. Through our daily prayers we are strengthened through faith to bear our daily troubles because it is the will of our Lord, Jesus Christ.

Sometimes it may seem that there is nothing being added unto you and that is because you are not focusing on what

God is giving according to what you need but focused on what you want. No one knows what we are in need of more than the Father Himself.

Because of our seeking the Kingdom of God our hearts are brought into subjection - the act or process of bringing someone or something under one's control to the will of God. His Kingdom in inside of you and you must lead others to the will of God through obedience of faith. We are no different from King Solomon who asked our God for wisdom and knowledge but received so much more. *Delight thyself also in the LORD: and he shall give thee the desires of thine heart.* Psalm 37:4 The most precious gift that we will receive when we seek His Kingdom is the gift of Salvation. To us it may seem like our Salvation is free but it is not because it came at a cost that could never be repaid and that was the life of Christ on the cross. Our acceptance of Salvation gives us a chance of living with Christ in heaven. *Surely he hath borne our griefs, and carried our sorrows: yet we did esteem him stricken, smitten of God, and afflicted.*

5 But he was wounded for our transgressions, he was bruised for our iniquities: the chastisement of our peace was upon him; and with his stripes we are healed. Isaiah 53:4-5

Now don't get it twisted that just because you seek the Kingdom of God and accept His Salvation that everything is going to be A-Okay, wrong. This is an insurance policy that you hold knowing that God will never leave you nor forsake you if you put Him first. Just like an insurance policy, in order to get something from the policy you have to make regular payments. To keep our walk faithful to God we must continue to read and study His word so we can get the blessings that He has promised. Nobody's perfect but He does expect us to do His will and not our own.

For those that are reading this and have not put God first in your life and would like to start today, follow the scriptures listed below.

So then faith cometh by hearing, and hearing by the word of God. Romans 10:17

But without faith it is impossible to please him: for he that cometh to God must believe that he is, and that he is a rewarder of them that diligently seek him. Hebrews 11:6

I tell you, Nay: but, except ye repent, ye shall all likewise perish. Luke 13:3

Whosoever therefore shall confess me before men, him will I confess also before my Father which is in heaven. Matthew 10:32

That if thou shalt confess with thy mouth the Lord Jesus, and shalt believe in thine heart that God hath raised him from the dead, thou shalt be saved. Romans 10:9

Then Peter said unto them, Repent, and be baptized every one of you in the name of Jesus Christ for the remission of sins, and ye shall receive the gift of the Holy Ghost. Acts 2:38

Printed in the United States
By Bookmasters